CW00670384

RUNCORN

THROUGH THE AGES

Jean & John Bradburn

AMBERLEY PUBLISHING

First published 2014

Amberley Publishing
The Hill, Stroud, Gloucestershire, GL5 4EP
www.amberley-books.com

Copyright © Jean & John Bradburn, 2014

The right of Jean & John Bradburn to be identified
as the Authors of this work has been asserted
in accordance with the Copyrights, Designs and
Patents Act 1988.

ISBN 978 1 4456 3864 5 (print)
ISBN 978 1 4456 3881 2 (ebook)

British Library Cataloguing in Publication Data.
A catalogue record for this book is available from
the British Library.

Typesetting by Amberley Publishing.
Printed in the UK.

INTRODUCTION

In 2015, Runcorn will celebrate 1,100 years of history. The Historical Society will be commemorating this in style.

In the tenth century, the area was in the Saxon Kingdom of Mercia. King Alfred had died in 899 and the responsibility of defending Mercia against the Vikings fell to his son, Edward, and his sister. Ethelfleda established a fort and a Christian chapel in Runcorn.

The next century brought the Normans. William's defeat of Harold brought about great change. The Norman lords inherited the land, and Norman bishops replaced the local clergy. Another significant point in the history of Runcorn is the foundation of the priory at Runcorn and its removal to Norton.

The Barons of Halton held the valuable fishing rights in the Mersey. They also controlled the crossing of the river. Most people had to swim across, or wait for low tide and take the risk. In about 1178, a ferry was established by John Fitz Richard, the sixth baron.

By the end of the thirteenth century, Halton was a place of some importance. The stone castle was complete. This provided a fine place to entertain in style. The surrounding countryside provided a deer park for the Lord of the Manor and his hunting parties to use. This came to an end with the siege of the castle in the Civil War.

The Duke of Bridgewater brought about the greatest change for Runcorn, with the coming of his canal. This was followed by the birth of industrial Runcorn. The last 100 years brought about a new crossing and the Runcorn New Town. This century will see a second road bridge to cross the Mersey.

BIBLIOGRAPHY

Cowan, Alex, *Last Orders.*
Cowan, Alex, *Time Gentleman Please.*
Howard, Liz, *The Way We Were.*
Nickson, Charles, *History of Runcorn*
Scribes and Scribblers, *Worsley to Top Locks.*
Starkey, H.F., *Old Runcorn.*

ACKNOWLEDGEMENTS

We must first thank Roy Gough. He published the successful *Runcorn Through Time* and was invited by Amberley to publish a second volume. He kindly asked us to undertake this. Thank you for giving us permission to use some of your photographs. We must also thank Alex Cowan and the Runcorn and District Historical Society. He was extremely generous with their photograph collection and his vast knowledge of the history of Runcorn. Thanks also to Evelyn Hayes for her kind advice.

ABOUT THE AUTHORS

Jean managed the local history collection in Runcorn and Widnes library for many years. She has also created the image website for Halton (www.picturehalton.gov.uk). She has published a number of heritage walk leaflets for Halton Library Service. Recently retired, she is an adult tutor offering courses in family history.

John has numerous production credits in theatre, TV and film (Ex-BBC and Granada). He has worked mainly for the last decade in portrait, film and artscape photography. Previous publications include:*Widnes Through Time* and *Cheetham Hill, Crumpsall, Blackley and Moston Through Time.*

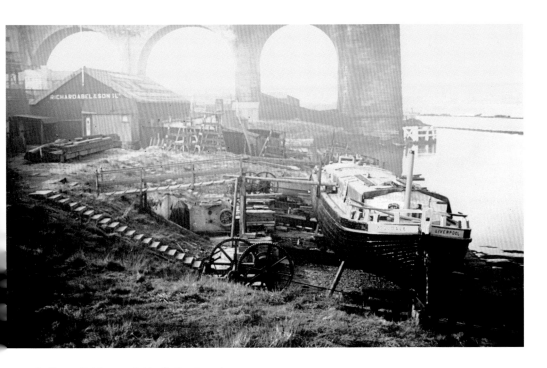

Railway Bridge and Abel's Boatyard

We can see the great arches of the railway bridge completed in 1868. It was while excavating the bridge that the remains of the ancient fort at Runcorn was discovered. It was built by Ethelfleda, daughter of King Alfred the Great, in 915. Richard Abel is first listed as a sail maker and canal carrier at Top Locks in 1892. By 1914, he was coming up in the world and was now a barge and tug owner, contractor and sand merchant based here at Castle Rock. The business flourished in Runcorn for over seventy years. The site was purchased for the building of the road bridge and closed around 1958.

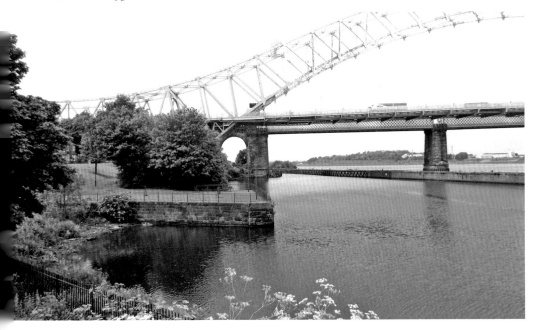

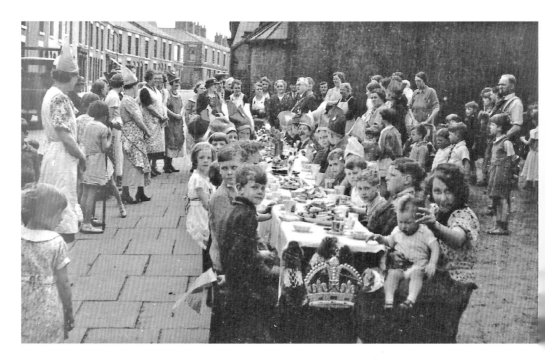

Ashridge Street Coronation, 1937

A street party to celebrate the Coronation of George VI and his wife, Elizabeth, in May 1937. This event would not have taken place if his brother, Edward, had not abdicated. It shows the community spirit that would hold them in good stead for the dark days of the Second World War. Some of you will perhaps recognise yourself as a child? Regrettably, many of the houses were demolished with the coming of the new bridge. The modern photograph is taken from the corner of the Devonshire Hotel looking down towards the Spiritualist church.

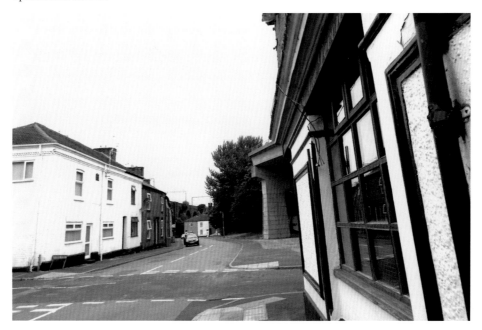

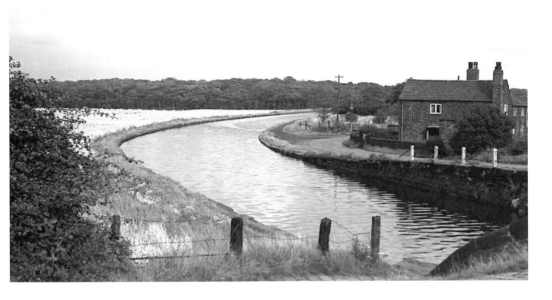

Astmoor Canal Scene

A tranquil scene by the canal as it was then and now, but Astmoor was the site of the busy Astmoor Tannery. It is said that the leather to make the Duke of Wellington's boots for the Napoleonic War was supplied from Astmoor. Great contributions were also made to the war effort during both world wars. By 1962, the tannery was closing, doomed by the advent of plastics.

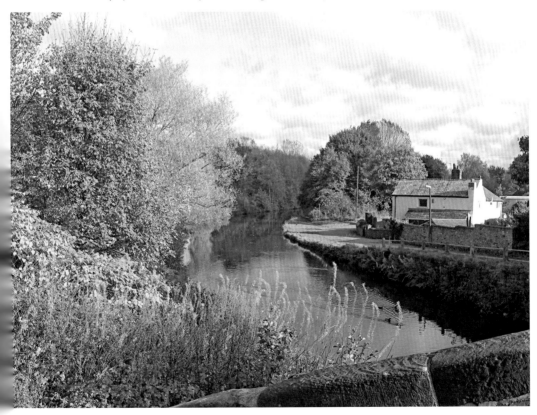

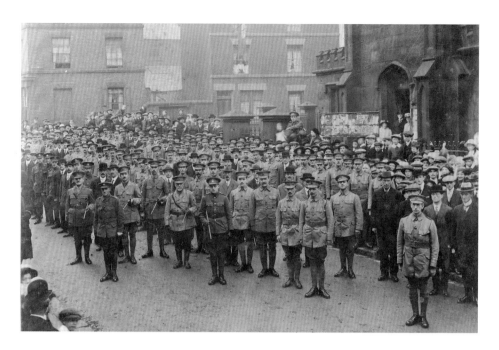

Bethesda/St Paul's Church Parade

In November 1916, Runcorn was proud to welcome the return of Thomas Alfred (Todger) Jones. He was awarded the VC for his outstanding bravery. Here we see the church parade in High Street. We can see the size of the crowds and the ladies watching from windows in Alcock Street. Major Timmins lead the parade, and stirring music was provided by The Highfield Band. Behind is Bethesda Chapel. Built of red sandstone, it was opened in 1835. Now we see the church parade leaving Saint Michael's church on 3 August 2014 to unveil his statute in the memorial gardens.

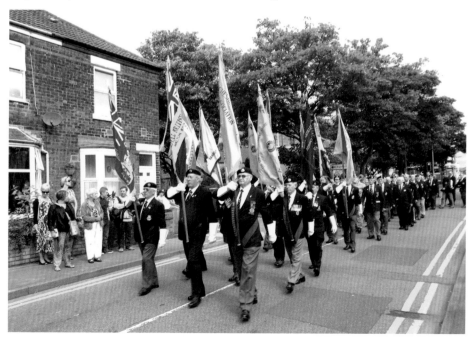

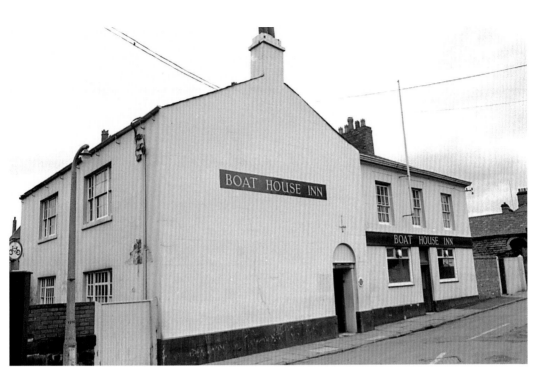

Boat House Inn

Hard to imagine now that this was a busy pub serving the employees from the Old Quay yard and the tug boat crews. It was originally called the Ferry Boat as it was located near the original ferry crossing. It was formerly old cottages, and was converted about 1760 into a public house. This view shows Mersey Road from across the river.

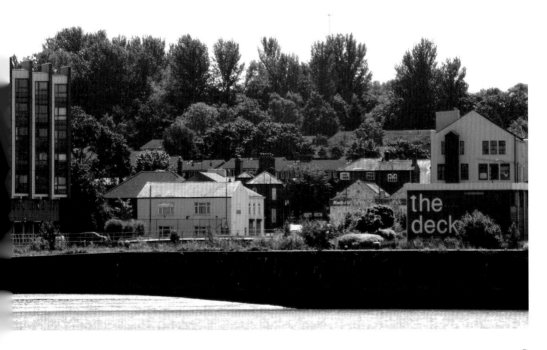

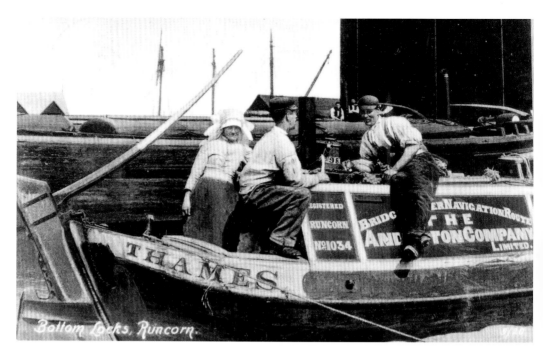

Bottom Locks, Runcorn.

Bottom Locks

As its name suggests, this was the last of the ten locks built by the Duke of Bridgewater coming down from Waterloo Bridge. Completed three months after the death of James Brindley, they were quite an attraction for sightseers. Here we see Joseph and Elizabeth Goode on *Thames* waiting for loading. She is wearing a traditional bargee headdress, worn to protect from sun and rain. When Joseph retired from the canal, he became an ostler in Percival Lane. Today, the area has been landscaped to show the line of the historic locks.

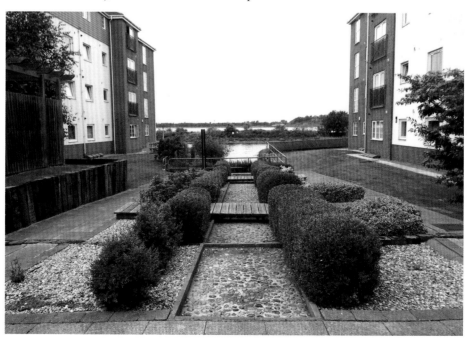

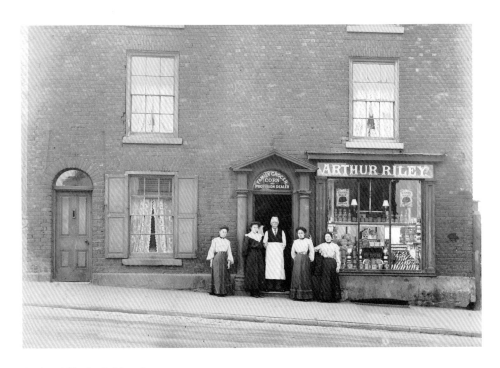

Arthur Riley's, Bridge Street

A thriving grocer and baker, Arthur was born in Weston in 1837. He opened his shop at Nos 47–49 Bridge Street with his wife, Elizabeth, as early as 1874. They had three daughters and three sons to help run the business. By the 1901 census, he was a widower. Happily, he still had his two daughters, Lily and Annie, to help him run the shop. The shop was still thriving in 1914, and was demolished in 1973. The large-scale map shows Bridge Street in 1874.

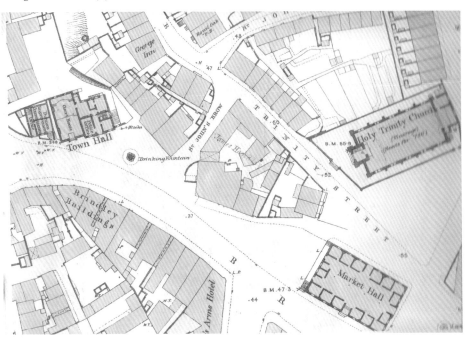

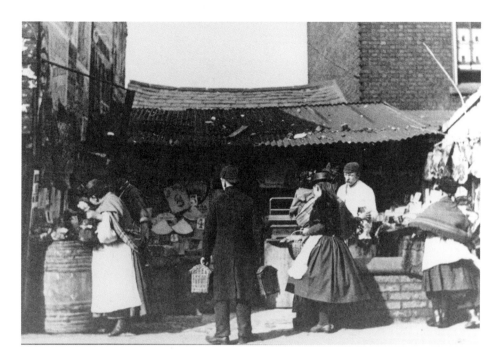

Bridge Street Market

Bridge Street was the location for the open market. Here we can see a stall in 1890. Runcorn did a good trade in pottery as the goods were transported up the canals from Stoke-on-Trent. Runcorn also boasted a fine market hall, opened in 1856. On the opening day, crowds rushed to see the fine gas lighting, not the excellent displays of meat, fish and poultry. We now see at the busy, outdoor market in Church Street.

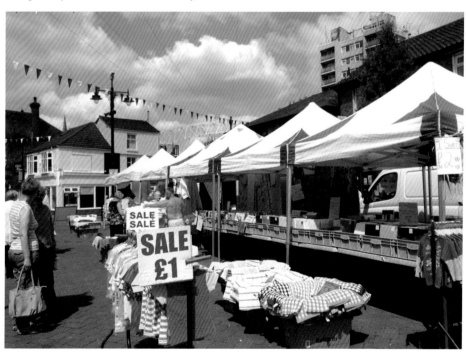

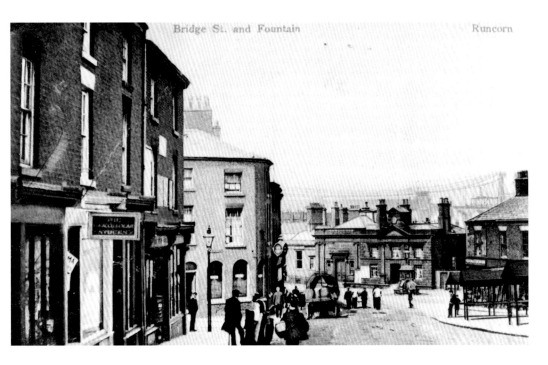

Bridge Street Fountain and Old Police Station

A lovely scene looking down Bridge Street towards the town hall and police station. It was built in 1831. The building was restored and reopened by the Queen in 1998. We can see a drinking-water fountain provided in 1857. It was removed in 1948. The market stalls are on the right, with Holy Trinity church and the Transporter Bridge beyond. The shops have all been demolished and were replaced with modern housing in 1975.

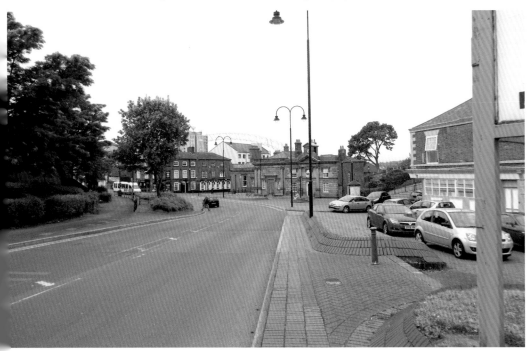

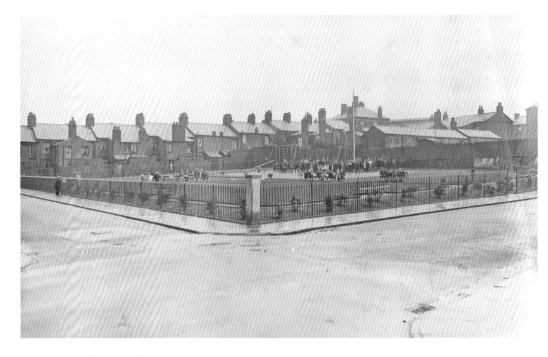

Holy Trinity Playground 1930s

The church was consecrated in 1838. Runcorn's population was growing fast and needed another church. The school was originally built as a Sunday school, but then became a school for all ages. It was on the corner of Pool Lane and Saint John's Street. What a pleasure it is to see the children filling the playground. The modern shot is of the children's playground on Parker Street, with the church behind hidden by trees.

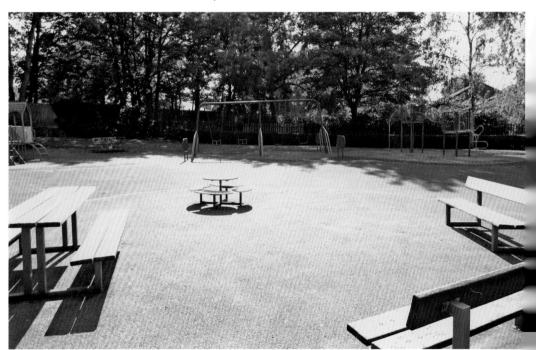

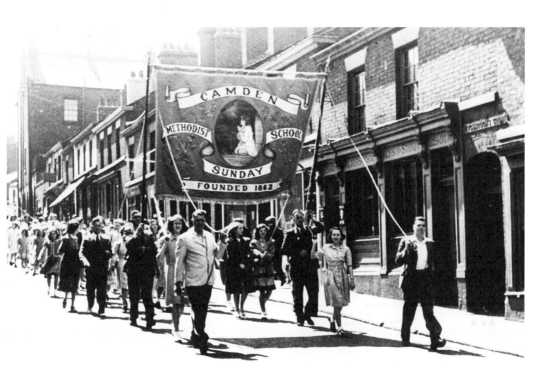

Camden Methodist

A Whit procession from Camden Methodist Sunday school walking down Regent Street in the 1960s. The church was built in Lowlands Road in 1862 by Thomas Hazlehurst. He contributed generously to Methodist chapels in Runcorn and beyond. Regent Street, as we can see, is still a shopping street.

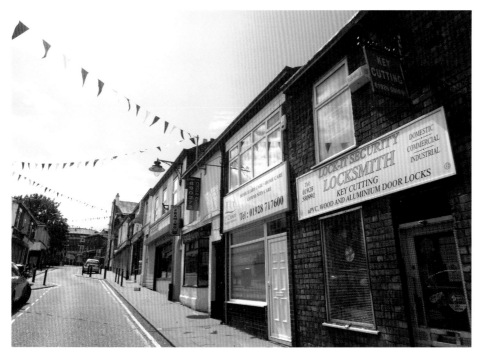

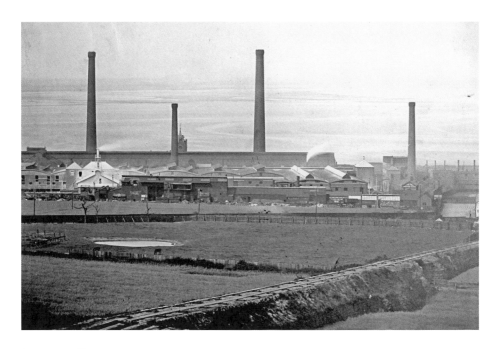

Castner Kellner

A shot from Weston Road showing the factory, and Drum Road from the quarries down to the docks. It was created in 1897 to manufacture caustic soda and bleaching powder. The name came from Hamilton Young, Castner of New York, and Carl Kellner of Vienna, who held the patents. In 1916, Castner-Kellner merged with Brunner-Mond, eventually forming ICI in 1926. The formation of ICI was an enormous boost for the local economy, and ICI became a much loved employer for many years. In 2001, ICI sold the Castner Kellner and Rocksavage chemical works to INEOS and, as we see, it is still thriving today.

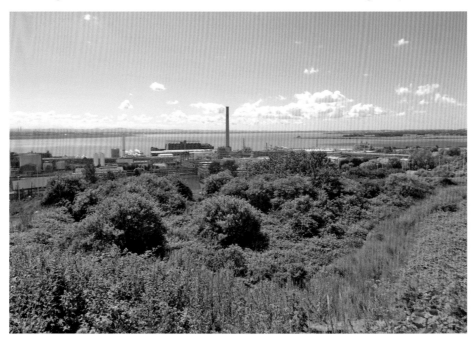

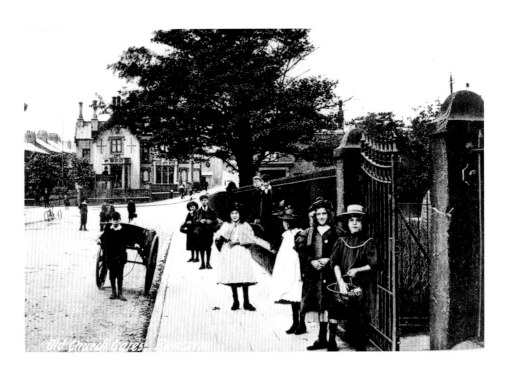

Church Street, c. 1900

A lovely photograph of children outside the church gates in Church Street. Beyond, we can see South Bank home of Dennis Brundrit. He was an eminent member of the town, a shipbuilder and stone merchant. He used his ships to transport Welsh granite to build the roads of Runcorn and beyond. It became a public house around 1890. Being so close to the Transporter Bridge, the hotel flourished until finally closing in 2006.

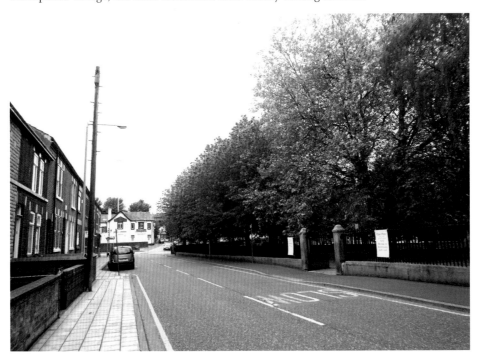

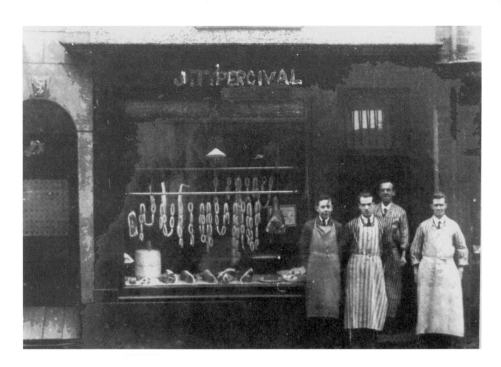

No. 69 Church Street, Percival's

George Percival opened the shop in 1874 with his wife, Elizabeth. He had three daughters and a son, Joseph. In front are Paul Handley, Marshal Hughes and George Wheat. By 1901, Joseph had taken over the shop at the young age of twenty-six. By 1911, he is still unmarried and living with his mother and his sister, Margaret, who both helped in the shop. His sausages were renowned throughout the town, and fame had clearly gone to his head as he was now described as a 'pork purveyor'. The original shop still stands in Church Street.

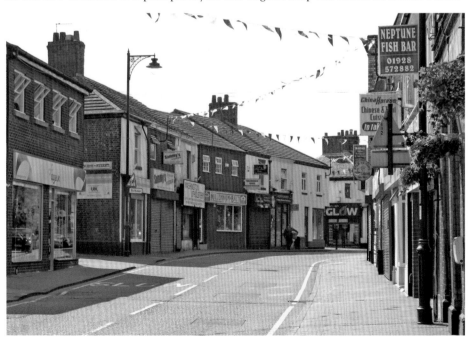

Crescent Row

This fine row was built in the mid-eighteenth century to house the porters and boatmen of the new Bridgewater Canal. Looking at the 1901 census, we can see that the residents were mainly working on the water; these included Joseph Hallsworth, lock keeper, and Joseph Wilding, barge waterman. Happily, these fine cottages still stand today. What a glorious flower display.

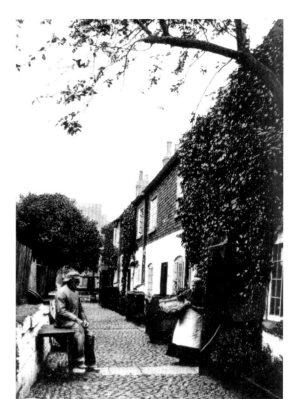

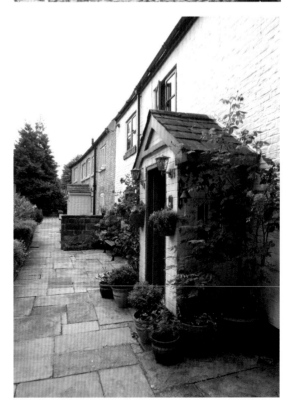

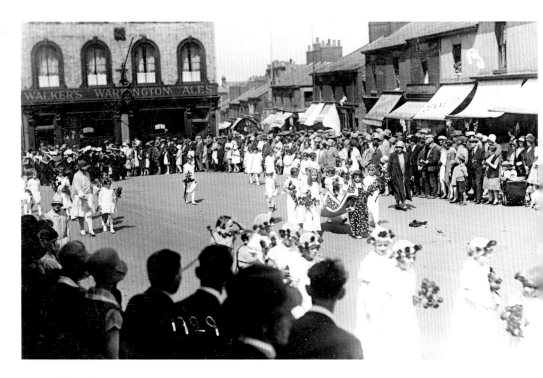

Devonshire Place

A lovely day for a parade in Devonshire Place in 1929. We can see Dennett's bootmakers and the bustling shops down Regent Street. Cross Street, on the right, is no more. We also see the Masonic Hotel that was built on the site of the old masonic lodge and assembly rooms. It is sadly now closed.

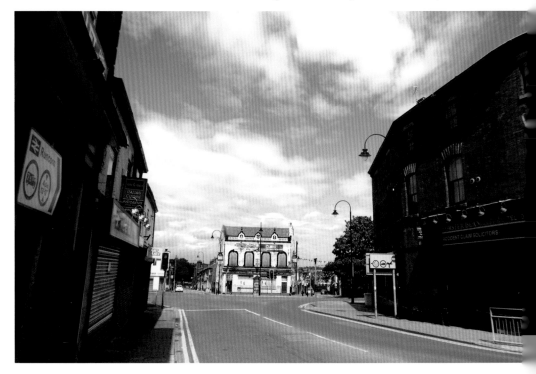

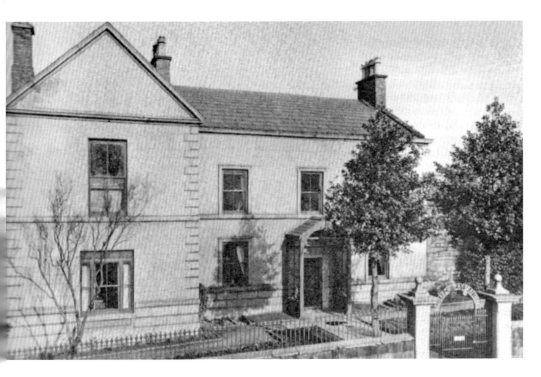

Crofton Lodge

Built in 1873, the Chadwick family of Daresbury lived here for many years. Later, Richard Abel and his family moved in. The house was sold to Evans, Lescher and Webb, who established a medical research institute here in 1902 in Westfield Road, close to the hospital. The works spread right across Westfield Road to Penn Lane.

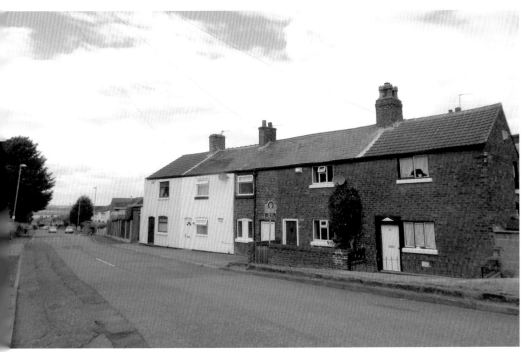

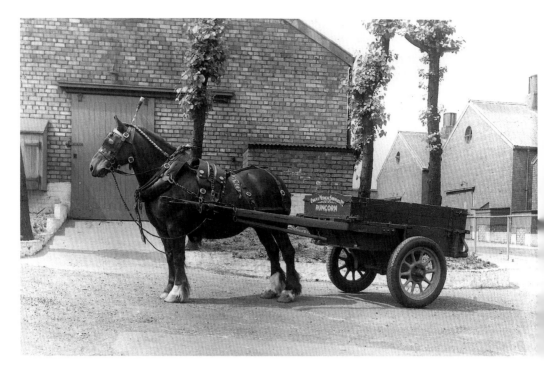

Evans Medical
A beautiful dray horse pulling the cart. During the First World War, Evans Medical opened Ellesmere Works in Gas Street to produce pharmaceuticals. Their pioneering work saved millions of lives worldwide. Evans Medical later moved from Runcorn to Speke, and was taken over by Glaxo.

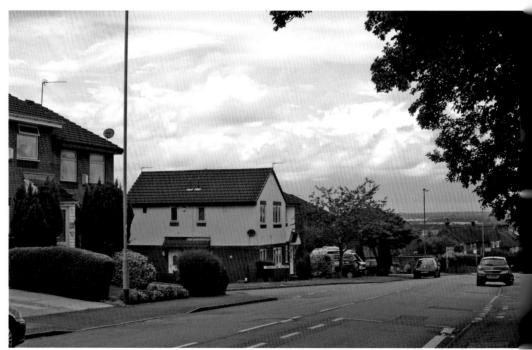

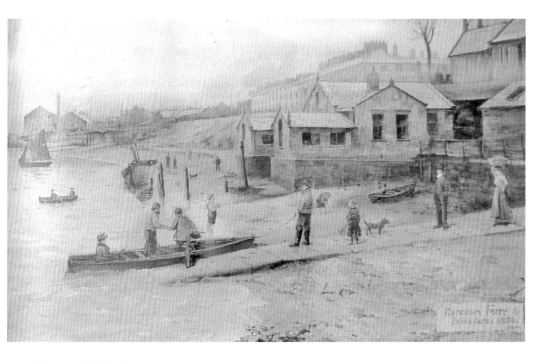

Ferry and Belvedere

An image from 1880 showing the ferry and Belvedere Terrace on the right. This fine terrace was built in 1831 to cater for the visitors to Runcorn who came to take the waters. The saltwater baths were built in 1822 on the river's edge below the church. Regency Runcorn became a popular place for the rich of Liverpool to visit, and even to send their children to boarding school. By 1835, there were a number of private schools in the town.

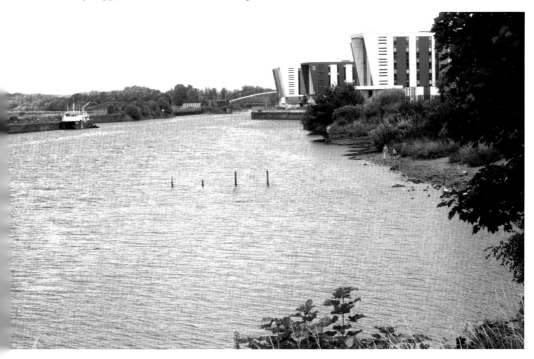

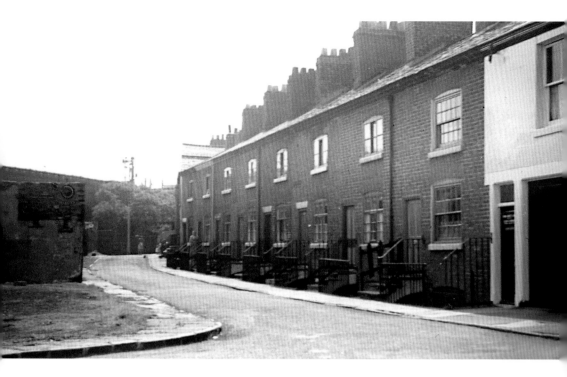

Gilbert Street

A view of Gilbert Street with the railway beyond. Originally, part of the street was known as Welsh Row. The street ran from Percival Lane, and we can see its position from the map, dated 1862. We can see the edge of the Bridgewater Arms, originally known as the Packet Inn; a popular name for pubs next to the canal. Gilbert Street, again, has been lost to new development.

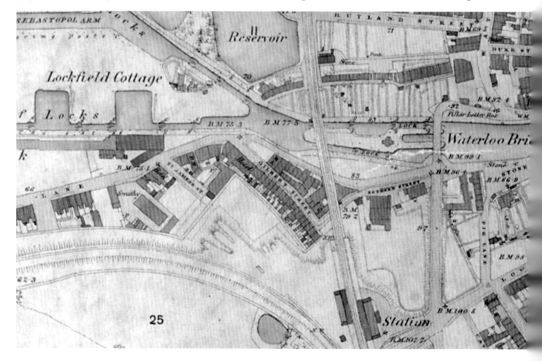

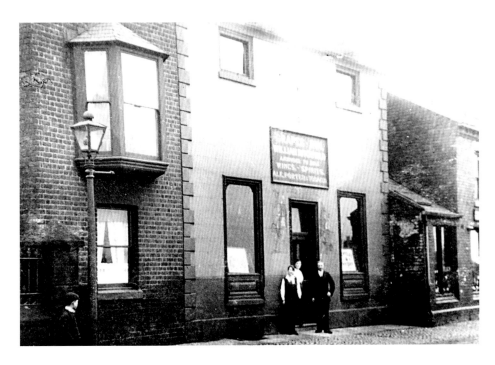

Grapes Inn

As we can see, the date of this photograph must be around 1916, when William Ditchfield was the landlord. The Ditchfield family were landlords of many Runcorn pubs. There was also a slaughterhouse behind the pub for a short time. In 1862, there was stabling for eight horses. It's now a café bar, and what optimism we felt for the English football team when we took this photograph. Sadly, things did not work out so well.

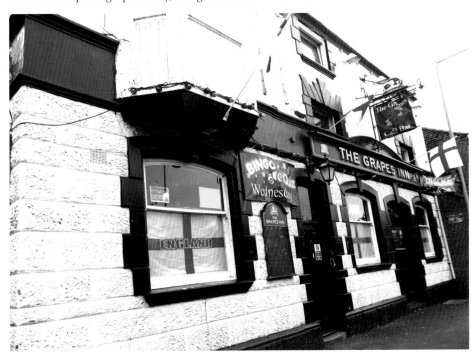

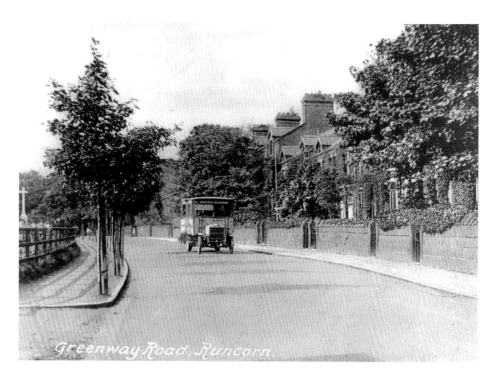

Greenway Road, 1920

We can see the war memorial on the left, now covered by trees in the modern shot. On the right, we see Stanley Villas, built around 1898 for the wealthy of the town. This area was known as 'Greenway Meadow', and in 1874, John Brundrit JP was living here. The houses still stand proudly today.

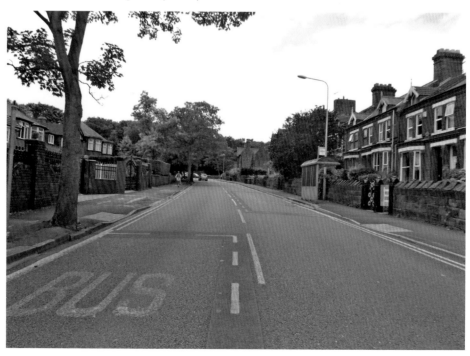

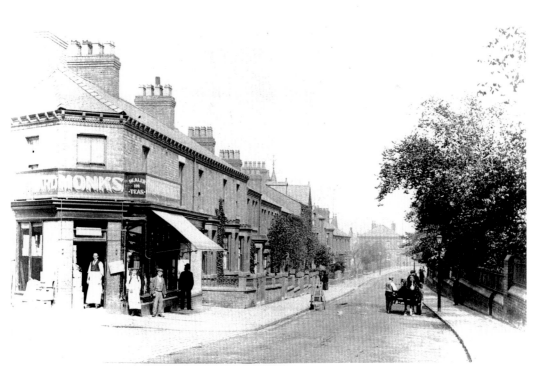

Greenway Road

A look down Greenway Road from Monk's corner, with Edward Monks proudly standing in the doorway. The Monks family have a long tradition of providing fine food in Runcorn. Edward's brother, Geoffrey, had a shop in Bridge Street. We had the great pleasure of meeting Geoffrey's son, Richard, still trading today. Here he is outside his shop in Granville Street.

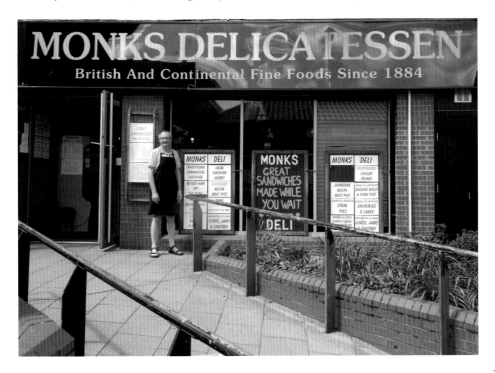

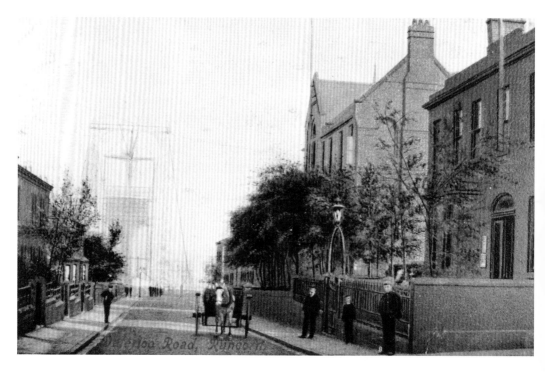

Waterloo Road

In the 1850s, Waterloo Road was a country lane leading to the ferry. Around it were the riverside villas such as South Bank and Grove House. The coming of the Transporter transformed Waterloo Road into a very busy street with passengers queuing. This encouraged shops to provide for the crowds. These are gone, and the road now is now much quieter.

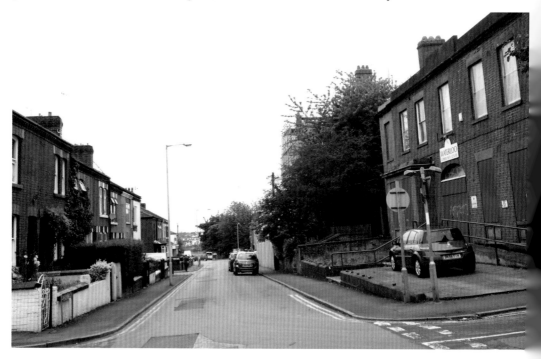

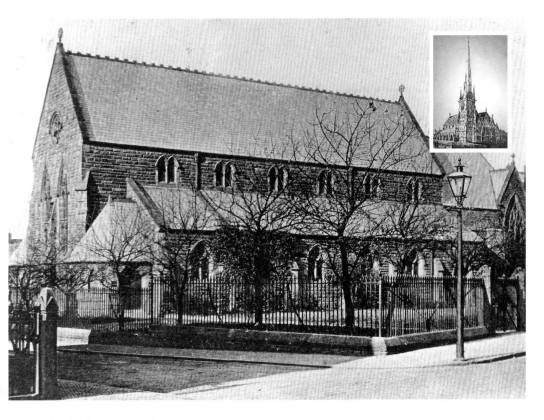

Saint Michael's Church
The greatly loved Canon Barclay did not live to see the opening of this church in Greenway Road. The church replaced the Newtown Mission in 1887, becoming an independent parish in 1931.This view of the architect's projection is how he intended it to look. Of course, the tower and the spire were never built.

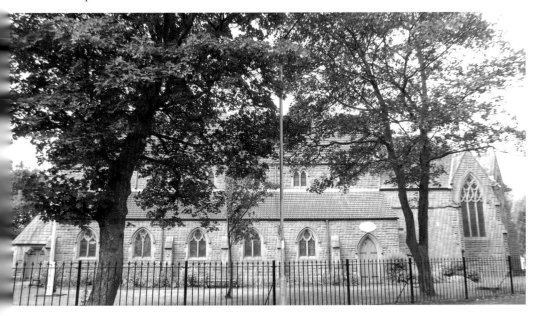

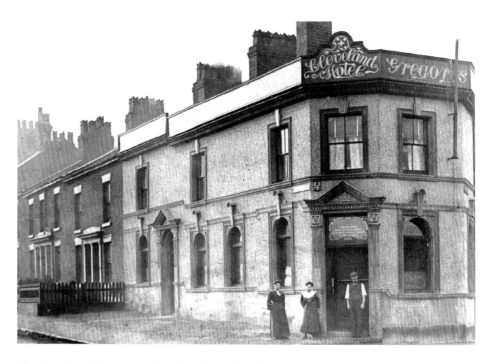

The Cleveland, Greenway Road/Lowlands Road

Standing on the corner of Greenway Road, this pub was first known as the Greenway Vaults. Here we see it around 1920. John Royle Hughes Garnett was the landlord from 1905–24. Perhaps this is him standing proudly at the door? Certainly, he knew his trade as he was landlord of Bridgewater Arms 1896–1903, and, later, The Railway and The Lion. It is a fine building, and it is sad that it does not stand today. We see the pub marked 'PH' on the map of 1862.

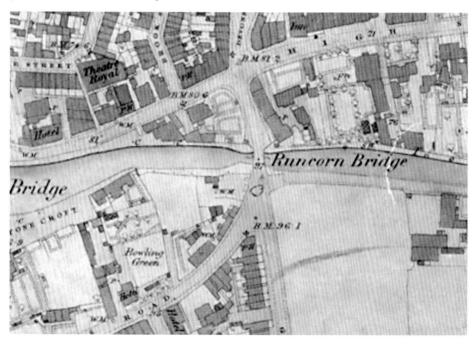

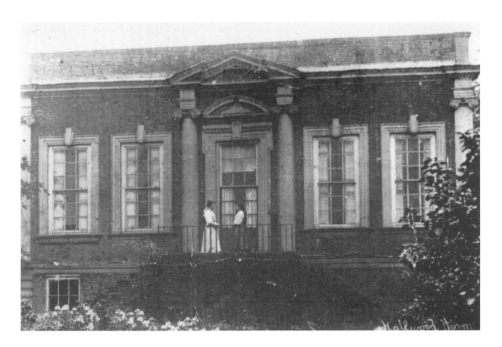

Hallwood

This was the home of Sir John Chesshyre, and was sadly demolished after bomb damage. The family were ardent Royalists, and suffered financial penalties when the Civil War was won by Cromwell. This mansion was built for Sir John Chesshyre around 1710. It was later used as a boys school. Mr Blake, the proprietor of The Hallwood Academy, was advertising in Liverpool newspapers from around 1815. We now see the Tricorn public house in Palacefields. The fine stables of the old hall still stand.

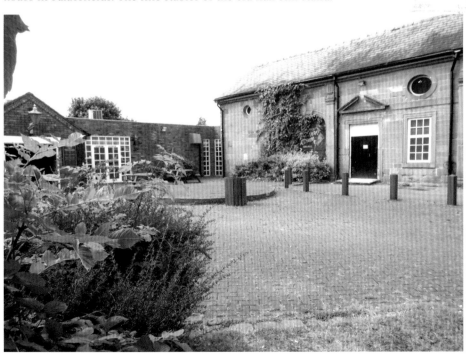

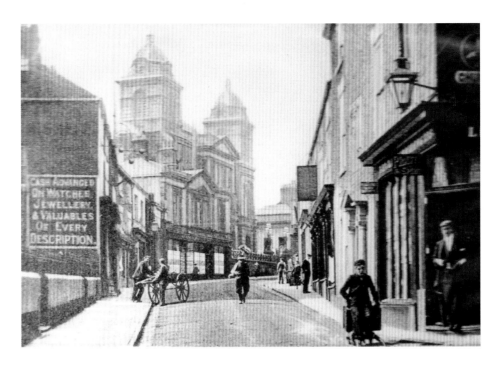

High Street, 1890s

Looking up from Church Street on the corner is Lightfoot's the pawnbrokers. At this time, when jobs were casual and there were many children to feed, the only way to pay the rent may have been to pawn a good coat or even a wedding ring. On the corner of Church Street we can see Lea & Sons Ironmongers. This was an old, established firm who also manufactured oxygen, hydrogen and nitrogen.

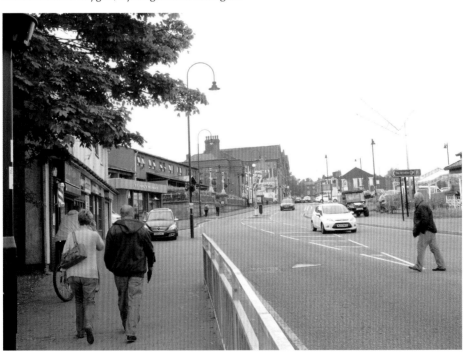

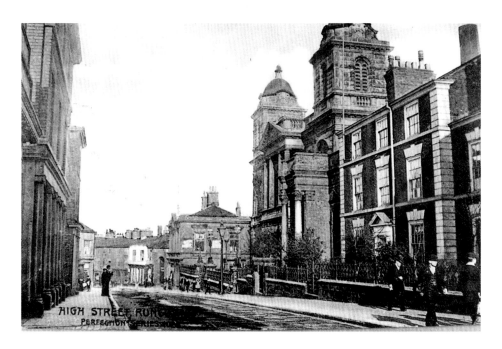

High Street, 1890s

Looking down towards St Paul's Wesleyan Methodist church. The handsome building with Italianate colonnades, balconies and towers was a church to be proud of, costing over £8,000. The church opened in November 1866. This was donated by Thomas Hazlehurst, the soap manufacturer and benefactor to the town. Its demolition in 1969 prompted Pevsner to declare 'the town has lost its one distinctive building'. We also see the fine Camden House, built in the eighteenth century. It is now a solicitor's. The bank and the health centre are beyond.

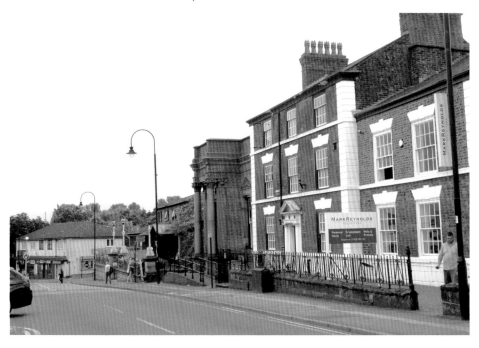

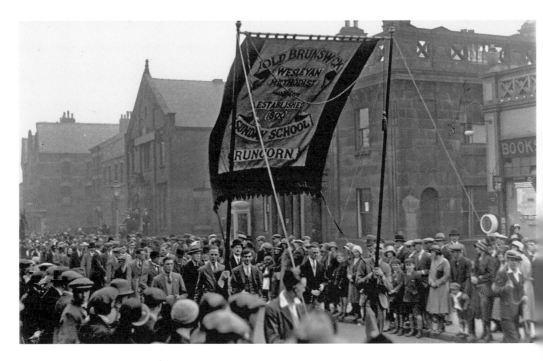

High Street

A Whit procession in High Street in around 1949. In the background we can see Bank Chambers and the Salvation Army Citadel. The Citadel was built on the site of the Old Hall, and during the war, it was an air raid wardens' post and the headquarters for the WVS. It was demolished in 1964, and is now Lloyds Bank. On the edge of the photograph we can see the Scala cinema that, regretfully, was demolished recently.

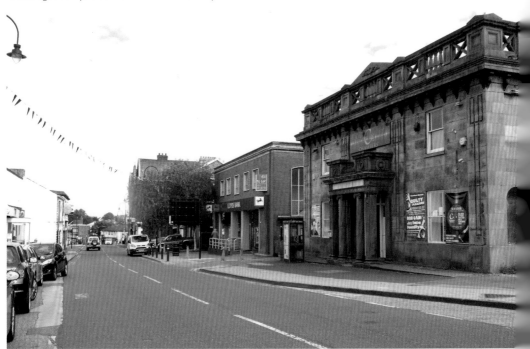

Halton Castle

Around 1070, the original wooden castle was built on the hill by Nigel 1st Baron Halton. Later, it was replaced by a stone castle. Although it was garrisoned by the Royalists in the Civil War, it fell to the Parliamentarians in July 1643. It was not well defended, and it was surrendered to Sir William Brereton, who held it until the powerful troops of Prince Rupert arrived. Royalists took it again, but it was lost once more to the Parliamentarians in 1644. It was then demolished to prevent further use.

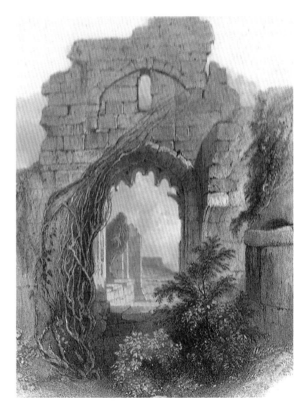

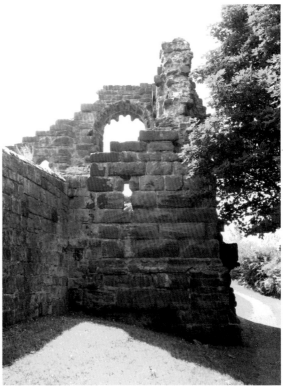

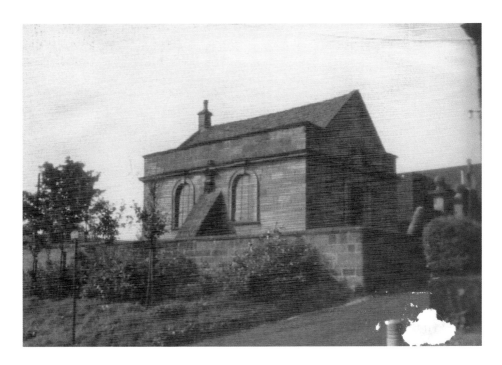

Chesshyre Library

Sir John Chesshyre built and endowed this library next to Saint Mary's in 1727. It is believed to be one of the earliest free libraries in England, built for the use of the gentlemen of Halton. It is the responsibility of the Vicar of Saint Mary's. The library was renovated and reopened by Hubert Chesshyre, an ancestor of Sir John's, in 1976. Many of the original books are still on display.

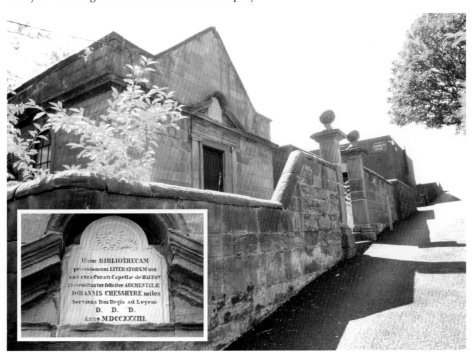

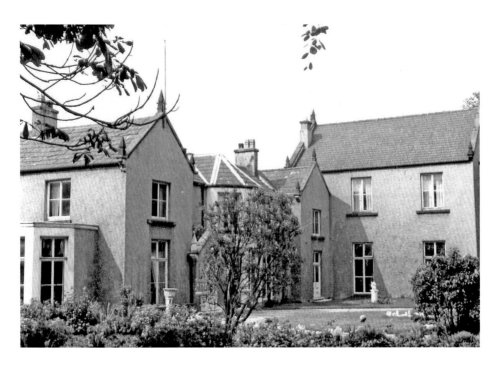

Halton Lodge

Another fine building lost to Runcorn. After the collapse of the Johnson Brothers' business, Charles Wigg bought Grice's farm from the Johnson's in Halton. A new house, Halton Lodge, was built for him. By 1871, he had moved back to Great Crosby. It was known locally as Grice's Farm. The family farmed here for many years. The house was on the site of Halton Lodge Primary School in Grangeway.

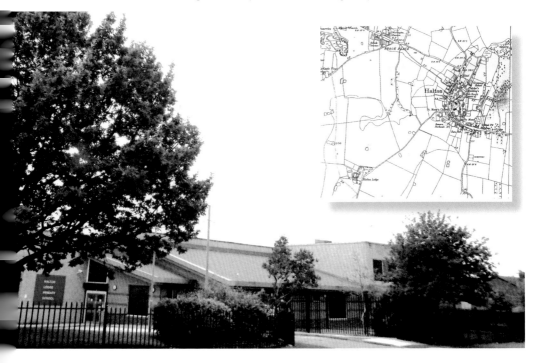

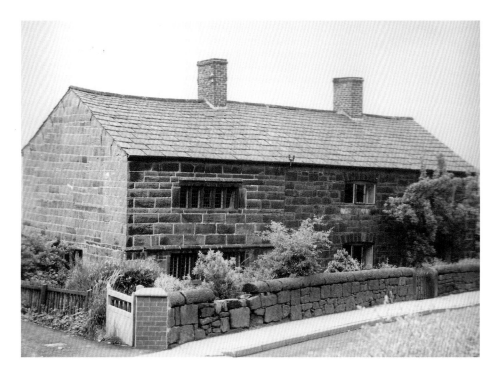

Halton Farm

A village farmhouse built in the early seventeenth century; it is a grade II listed building. Built in local sandstone, the farmhouse has mullion windows that contain leaded lights at first-floor level. Above the first floor, the windows are string courses. The tithe map of 1836 shows it to be the property of Sir Richard Brooke.

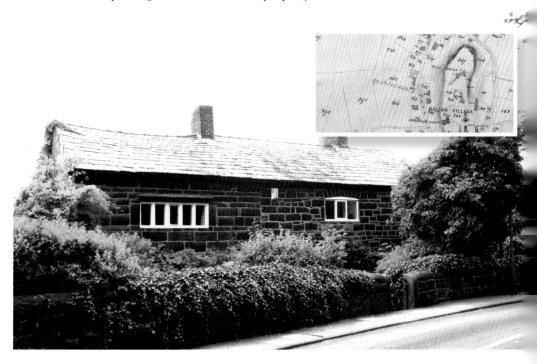

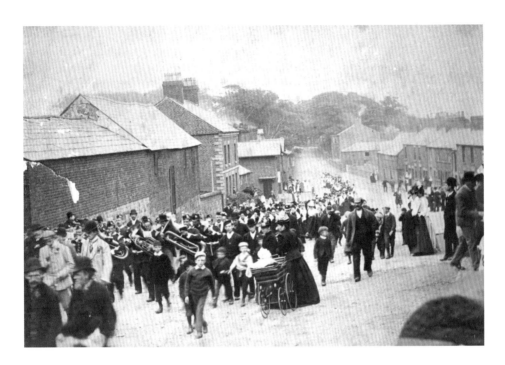

Main Street Halton

A Whit procession in Main Street, taken from Halton Trinity Methodist church, again built by Thomas Hazlehurst, and opened in 1875. This is the only one of twelve Methodist chapels built by him that is still in use as a chapel. We can see the fine house and the almshouses, dated 1827, that were built for the retired servants of the Brooke family of Norton Priory. With the thriving village shop, it is still a fine scene today.

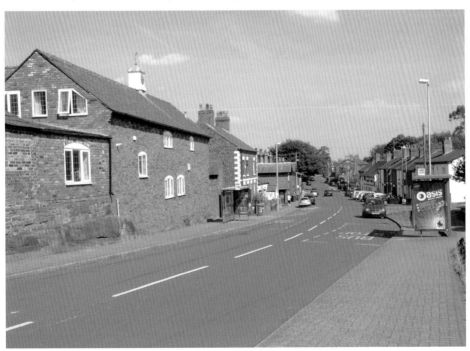

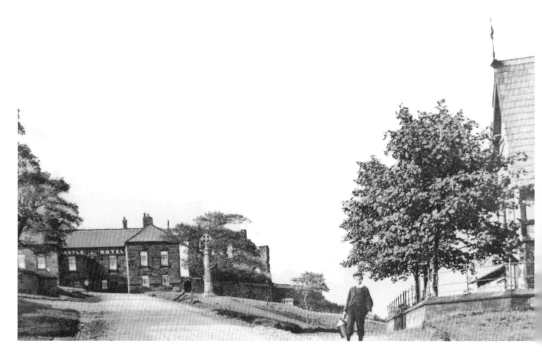

Castle Hotel

This building was originally integrated into the walls of the castle and used as a court house. It was built of local sandstone with a slate roof. The courtroom was on the first floor, and prisoners were housed in the cellars. The entrance to the court room was approached by an external stone staircase, and its door case is surmounted by the royal arms. It is now a public house. We can see the memorial in front, in celebration of the men of Halton who returned safely from the Boer War (1899–1903). We can just see Hill House on the right.

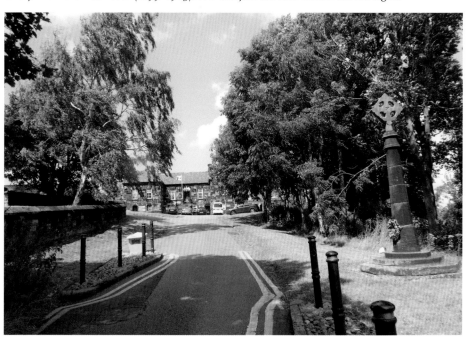

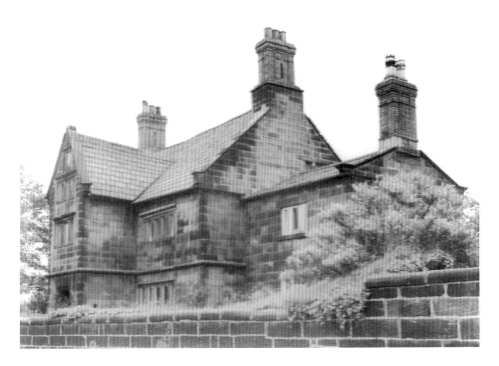

Halton Old Hall, 1693

Halton Village is fortunate to still have several Jacobean houses still standing. The Old Hall on Halton Common is dated 1693, but is built in a much earlier style. The house was rebuilt after having been damaged in the Civil War. A two-storey wing was later added to the north. The house has mullion windows and a studded door. Today, it has a sombre look to it. Let's hope someone brings it back to life!

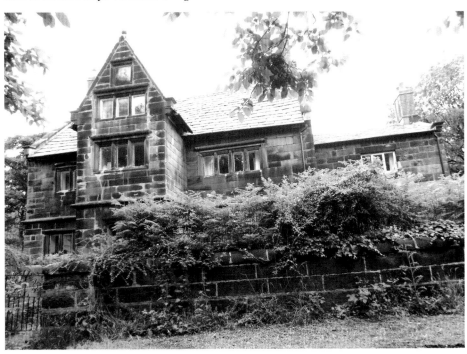

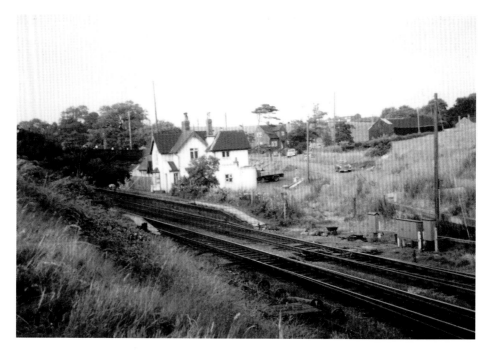

Halton Station

Halton station was on the Warrington and Chester line that opened in December 1850. There was a fatal accident in the Sutton Tunnel in April 1851. It was Chester Cup Day, and the line was exceptionally busy. The leading train did not have lamps fitted to the rear and was hit from behind. Being in a fairly isolated location, the line was never very busy. It did not survive long after the nationalisation of Britain's railways in 1948, closing to passengers in 1952 and to goods in 1954. The station house is now a private residence.

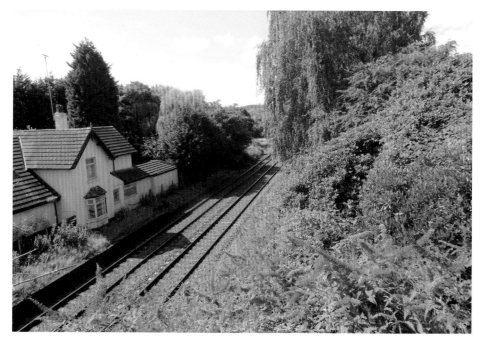

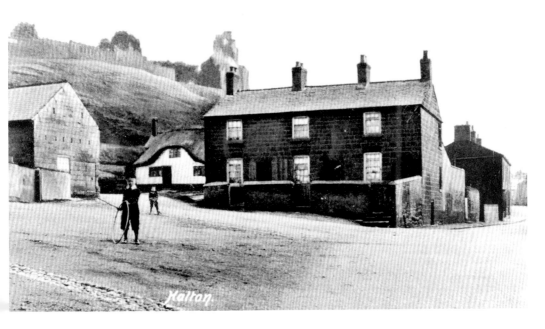

Halton Village

This charming photograph of children playing with a hoop shows the cottages opposite The Norton Arms, Main Street, and the castle up the hill. The fine, thatched cottage is now gone. Thankfully, Halton Village, with its fine sandstone buildings and its unique history, is a designated conservation area.

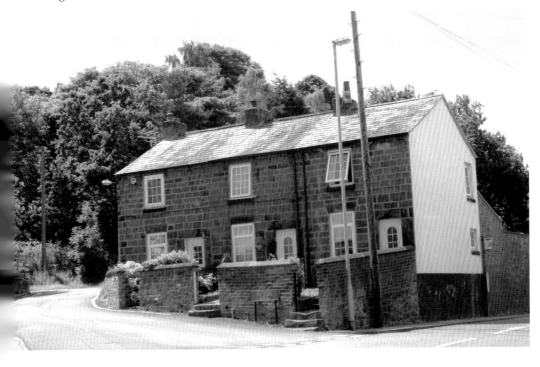

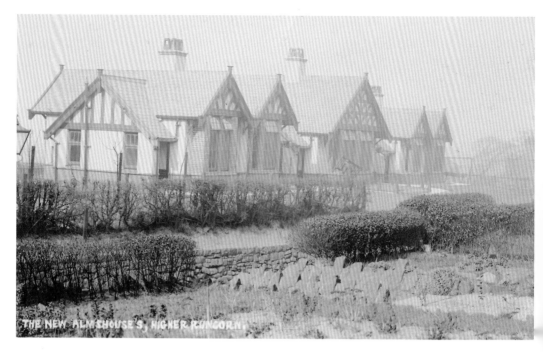

THE NEW ALMSHOUSE'S, HIGHER RUNCORN.

Higher Runcorn Citizens' Homes

These fine homes on Holloway were designed by James Wilding, Surveyor to the UDC. He was responsible for many fine buildings in Runcorn, including Egerton Street Library and the cottage hospital. The homes were built in the hospital grounds in 1910. They were vested in the council and were the gift of Sir Frederick J. Norman, chemist of the United Alkali Company and local philanthropist. Was it he who inscribed the quotation, 'What I spent I had, what I saved I lost, what I gave I have'?

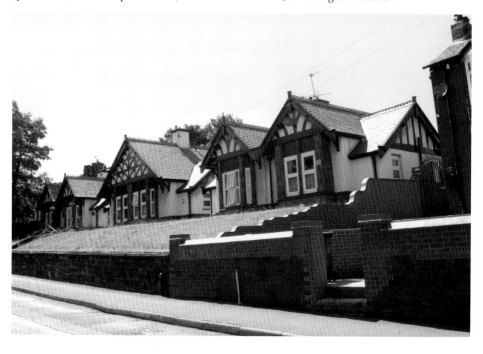

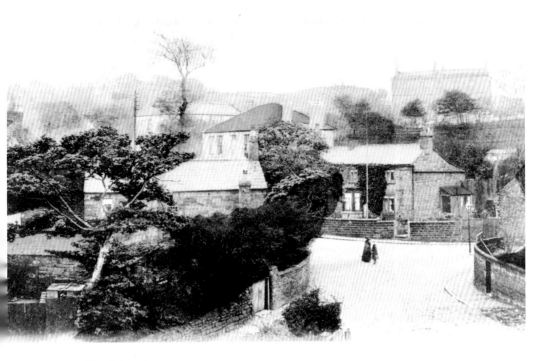

Beacon Hill, Higher Runcorn

This charming photograph was taken from beside the cottage hospital. We see Willesden Cottage, Westfield Road and Beacon Hill beyond. The fine house at the top is Rockfield, dating from around 1760. In 1914, it was the home of Charles Timmins. In 1939, it belonged to Norman Boswell, a well-known physician and surgeon in the town. Later it became the home of the Woodcock family.

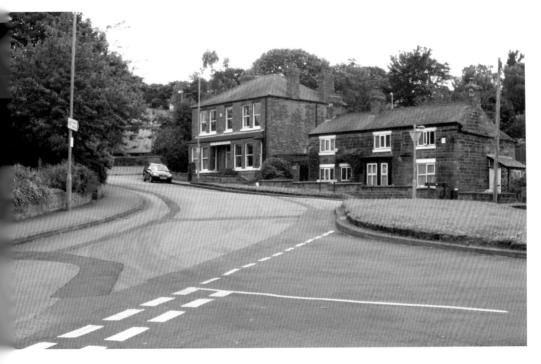

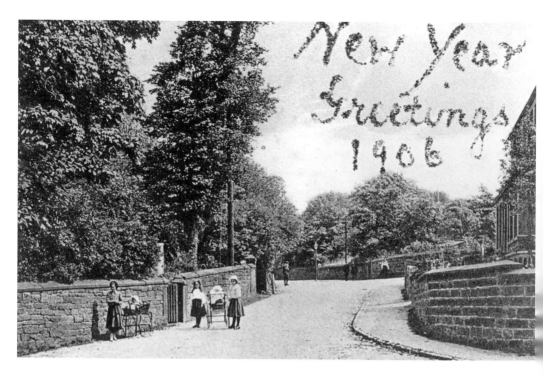

Holloway, Higher Runcorn

Another photograph taken in the early 1900s showing the same corner. Just on the right we can see 'Ingledene'. This was the home of Mrs Ann Abel, of shipbuilding fame, after the death of her husband, Richard. Opposite, on the left, we can just see Holloway Cottage, built in 1753.

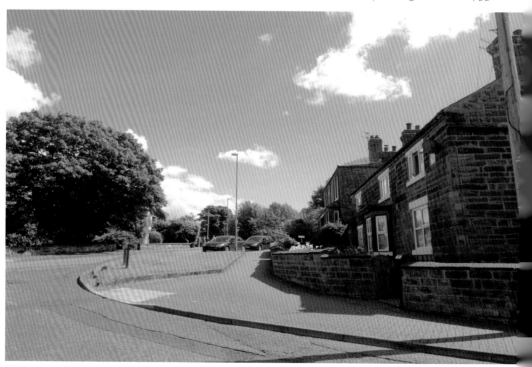

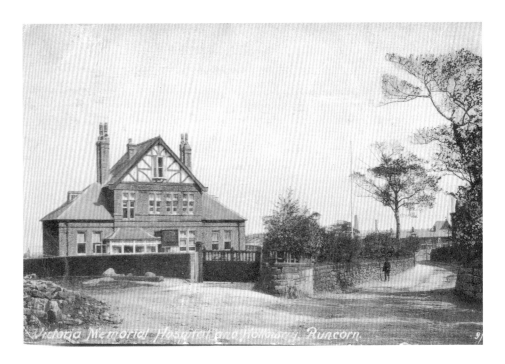

The Victoria Memorial Hospital

The hospital was built in 1903. It was known locally as the Cottage Hospital. It was a welcome facility for the town, providing beds for thirty-two patients and a large outpatients' department. Mr Simpson would come from Liverpool to perform surgery, visiting twice a week! There was no National Health Service as we know it today .The hospital was financed by generous support from the people of Runcorn.

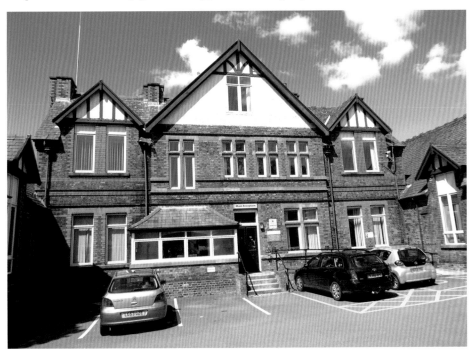

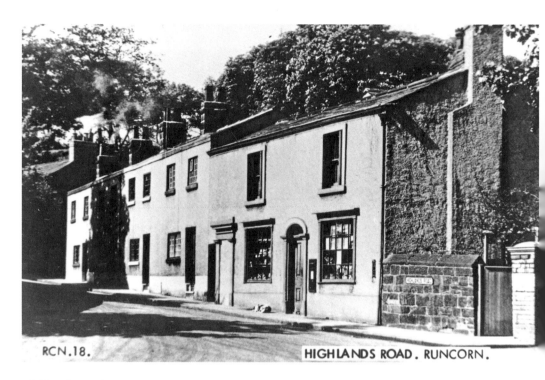

RCN.18.   HIGHLANDS ROAD. RUNCORN.

Highlands Road

The post office was situated on the corner of Highlands Road. Samuel Walker was the sub-postmaster in 1914. At this time, there were no fewer than four sub post offices in the town. The cottages next door have since been demolished. We now see Cheshire Bake House and tea rooms standing proudly on the corner.

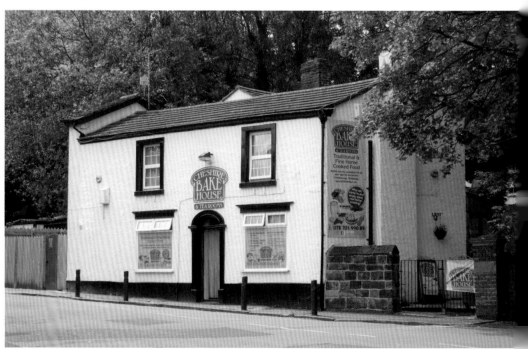

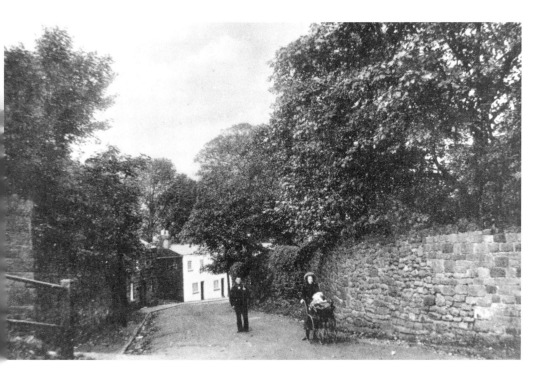

Highlands Road

This is quite a push up Highlands Road to Runcorn Hill, as this lady seems to have shopping, as well as the baby, in her pram. It looks quiet here, but Highlands Road must have been a very busy road as it led to the quarries on the hill. It is still a fine road today. The fine sandstone walls can still be seen.

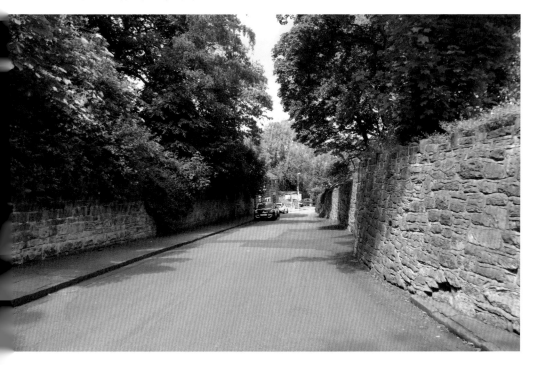

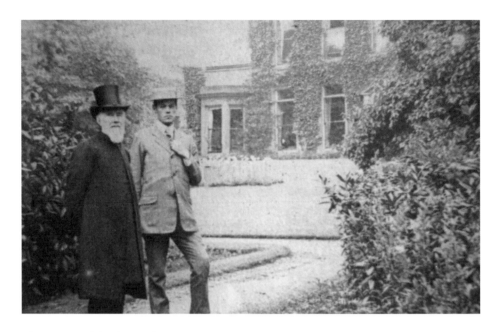

Vicarage, Highlands Road

Archdeacon Wood with a parishioner in the vicarage garden, around 1905. What a wonderful top hat he is wearing. The house was built in 1800. It was paid for by Vicar Keyt, possibly not to high standards, as by 1900, it was in a bad condition. The old vicarage was reached by a grand drive. The original gateposts are now at the entrance to the war memorial. The coach house is now the Vicarage Lodge nursery. Vicar Howard Perrin (later Canon Perrin) built a new house in 1912 on the same spot. During the First World War, the large vicarage was used as an auxiliary military hospital. Army huts were built in the garden. This new vicarage is once again the old vicarage as another house has been built below.

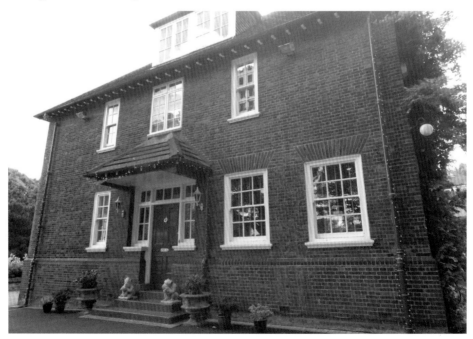

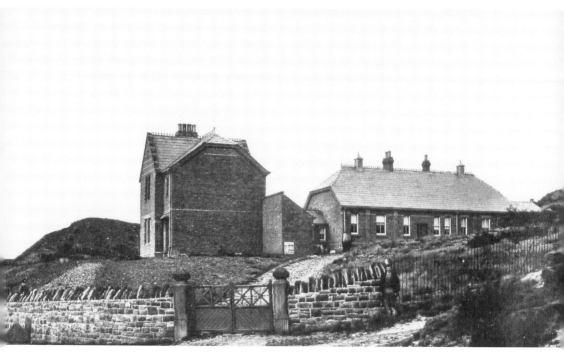

Isolation Hospital, Sandy Lane/Weston Road

Built in 1883 and known locally as the fever hospital, it was built to cater for the many outbreaks of smallpox, scarlet fever and diphtheria that were prevalent. Staff were prevented from leaving the grounds of the hospital to avoid transmission of disease into the town. Mrs Louisa Houlbrook was the matron in 1902. New homes are now on the site.

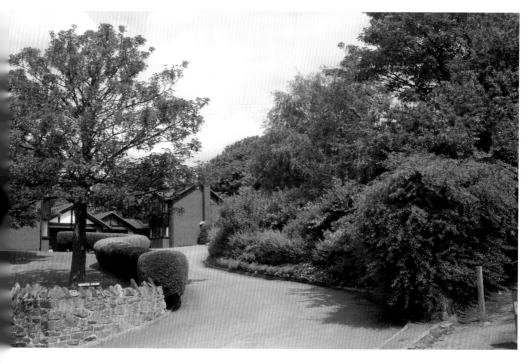

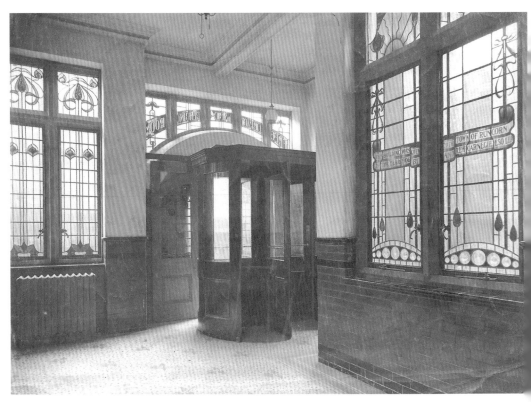

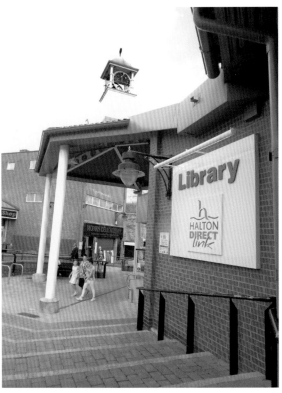

The Library, Egerton Street

This photograph of the library entrance must have been taken after 1906 as we can see the fine lettering praising the generosity of Andrew Carnegie, the great Scottish-American benefactor. He gave a grant of £3,000. The new library was built adjacent to Waterloo House. It was designed by James Wilding, surveyor and water engineer to the RUDC. The library closed in 2012 when a new library was opened in Granville Street. The old library is a listed building, and let's hope it can be preserved for the future.

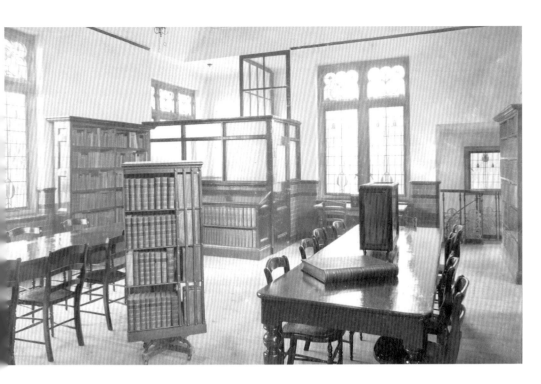

The Library Reference Room

The reference library upstairs at the Egerton Street site. It is hard to believe, but this once was state-of-the-art, and the open-plan shelves were a great innovation. The spiral staircase, though handsome, must have proved difficult to negotiate. The new library in Granville Street provides modern IT facilities and an information service for Halton Borough Council.

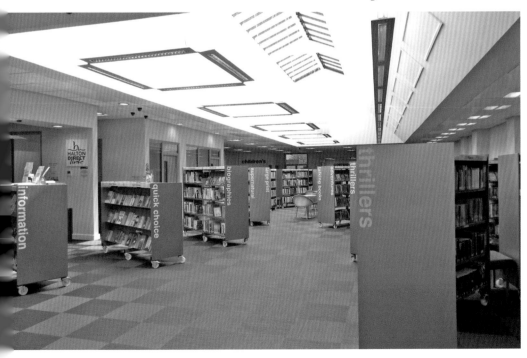

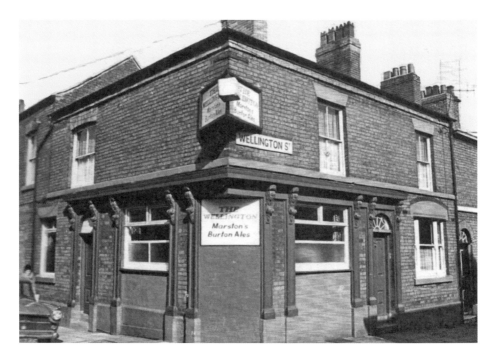

The Wellington

The Wellington Inn on the corner of Egerton Street and Wellington Street. The inn dates from as far back as 1857. Always a popular local pub for drinkers, with no pretensions of being both a pub and a hotel. Being next to Egerton Street library, it was the venue for library meetings before alcohol in the workplace was frowned upon. It has recently been renovated, and now looks very smart again.

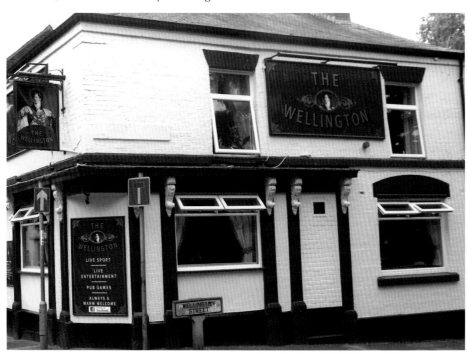

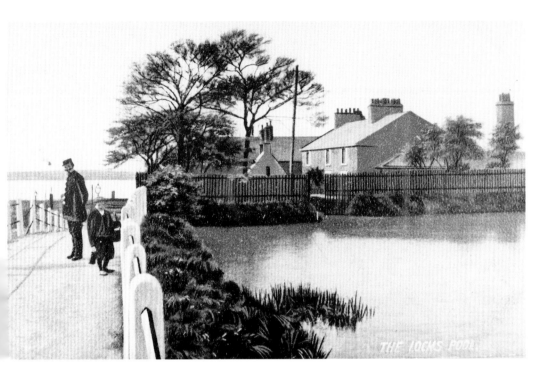

Locks Pool

A view looking down the locks to the Manchester Ship Canal. The pool acted as a local reservoir. Beyond, was the Custom House on the old Coach Road. It was built in 1847, when Runcorn became an independent port from Liverpool, and demolished in 1979. The pool, like the locks, have now been drained and provide a green open space.

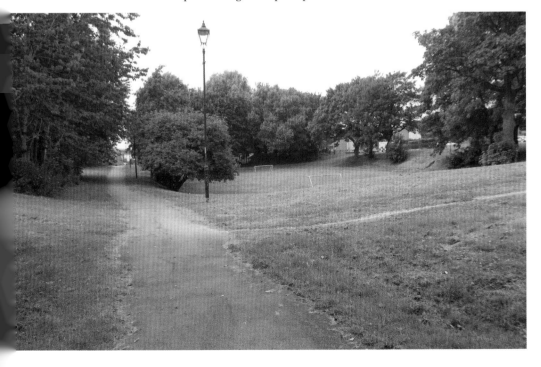

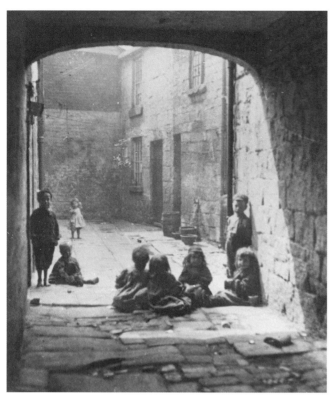

Lowe's Court, Off Cooper Street

This area, known as 'The Rookery', was an area of shabby, crowded and inadequate houses. Disease prospered because of the lack of drainage for sewage. They were often home to poor Irish immigrants. These tiny court dwellings were named after the landlords who profited from the rents. They were demolished in the 1950s, and we now see the fine homes built nearby.

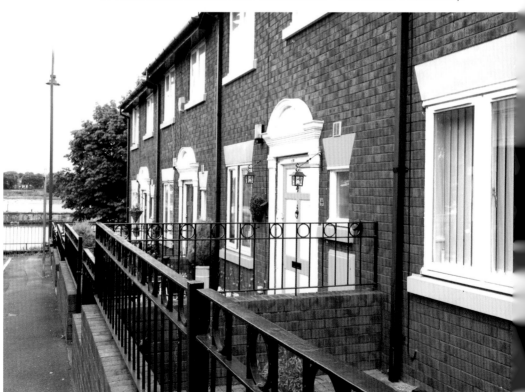

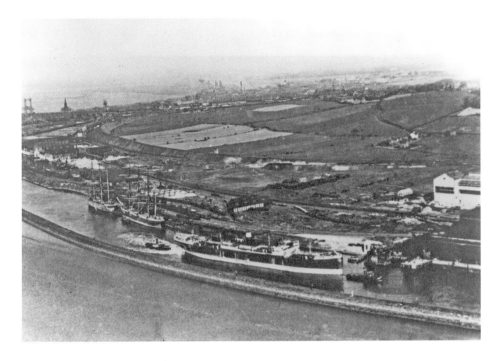

The Manchester Ship Canal

The building of the ship canal was said to be the greatest civil engineering project of the Victorian Age. A canal to bring shipping to the centre of Manchester must have seemed like a dream. Within six months of its opening, 630 vessels had headed up to Manchester from Runcorn. In 1911, the curve we see had to be widened to increase the tonnage of ships wanting to use the canal. Sadly, we no longer see many ships, but there are plans to bring the canal back to life as part of the Atlantic Gateway project. Below we see a shot from Pickering's Pasture showing the Mersey, with the canal in the distance.

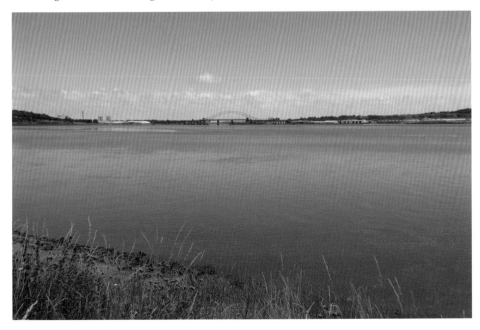

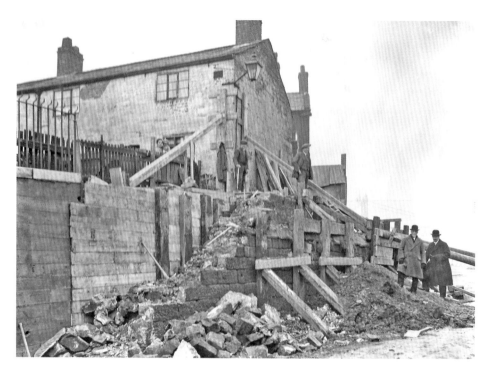

Mersey Road Widening, c. 1900

Demolition near to Mount Pleasant on Mersey Road. A mother and child are looking on with some apprehension (it looks like a health and safety nightmare). Could one of the men be James Wilding, surveyor to the UDC? They are not dressed for work, and look in some danger.

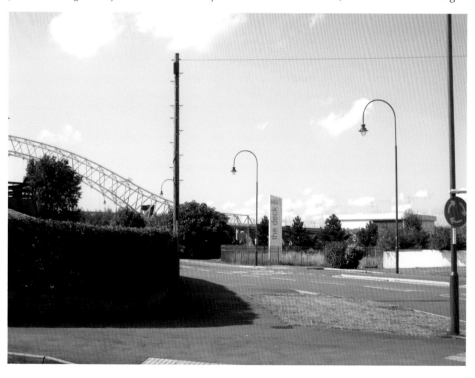

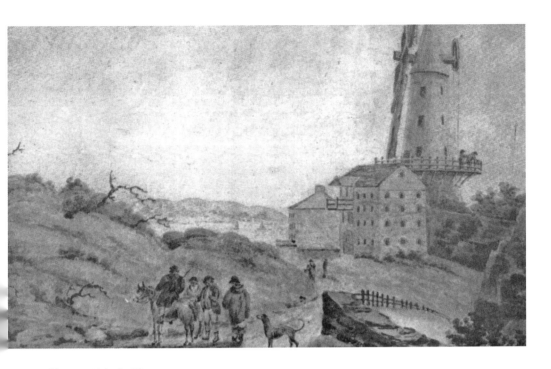

Mill Brow Windmill

When we first saw this image of a windmill, I assumed it to be up on Windmill Hill. But no, Nickson's *History of Runcorn* tells us there was a windmill here on Windmill Brow. This image is believed to show Leicester's Mill, which only ceased to operate with the arrival of steam power around 1861. Bagshaw's Directory of Runcorn, 1850, shows William Jepson, corn miller, at Mill Brow. The area was later quarried for its fine sandstone, and now the area has become a public park known as 'Rock Park'.

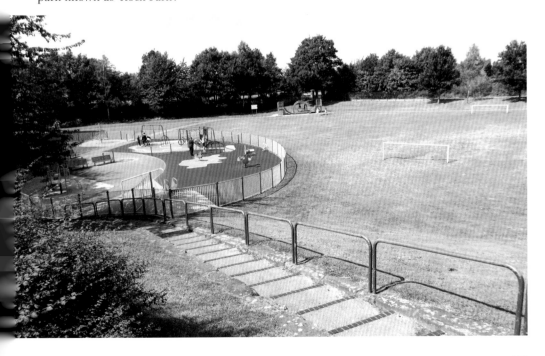

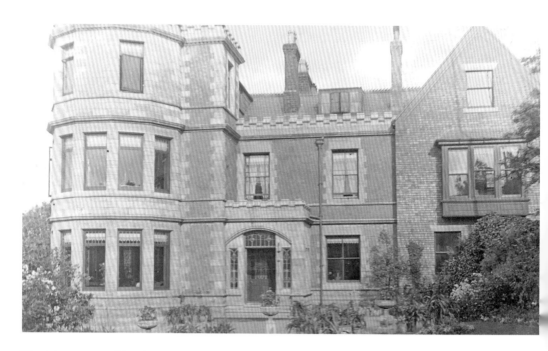

The Mount, Moughland Lane

Always an affluent home. In 1881, George Wigg, the son of Charles of the famous alkali works, lived here with his wife, Lilian, two daughters, and one son. By 1901, Robert Posnett from Camden Tannery had made it his home. Sadly, it has now been demolished and turned into a fine housing development called 'Southlands Court'.

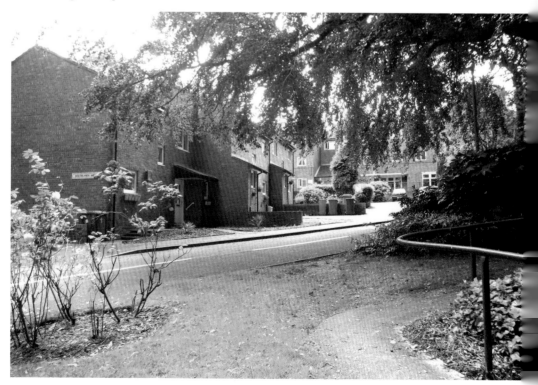

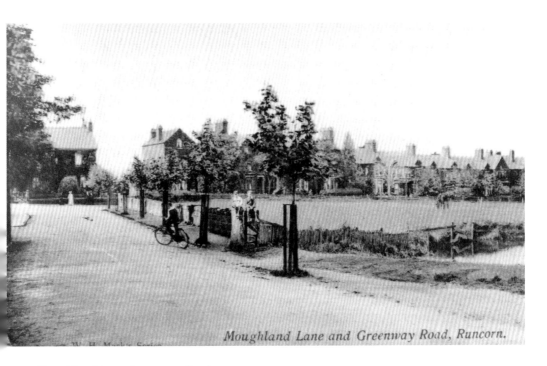

Moughland Lane and Greenway Road, Runcorn.

Moughland Lane Greenway Road

This would have been the scene from The Mount – horses in the field and the pleasant houses on Greenway Road. On the left, we see Greenway Cottage, built in 1869. The fine homes of Higher Runcorn were built for the prosperous businessmen who arrived in Runcorn. Living in Moughland Lane were Julius Raschen, consulting chemist at The Highlands, Harry Baker, chemist at Epsworth House, and William Rowland, steamship owner at Eversley.

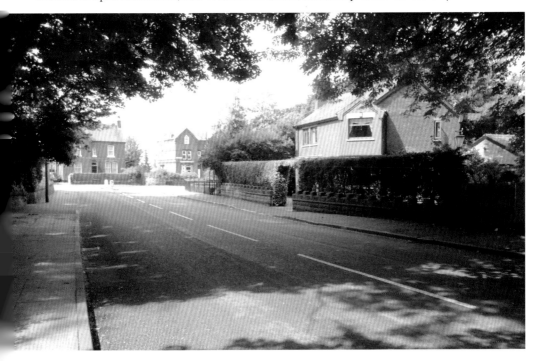

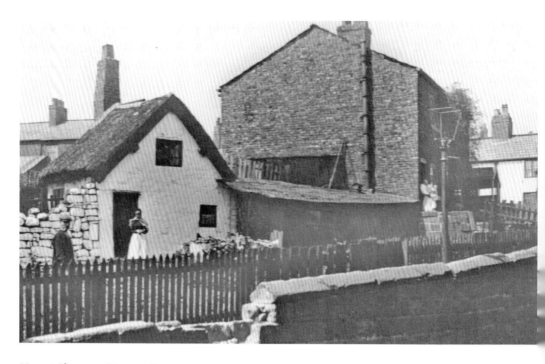

Mount Pleasant, Mersey Street

It has been claimed that Abbey Cottage, the oldest cottage in England, was built on Mount Pleasant. It was said to be lodgings for the friars visiting Runcorn. By 1901, the whole row was badly overcrowded. The men struggled to keep their families together on the wages of chemical labourers. The 1901 census shows John Cawley and his six children living here. The area has now been transformed.

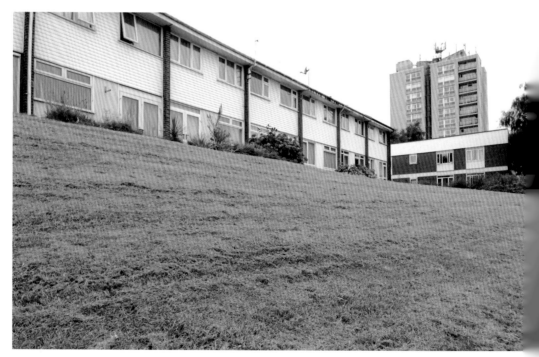

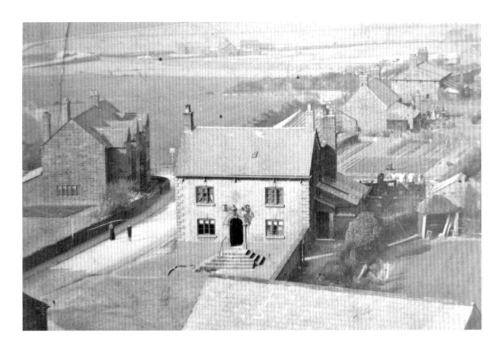

Norton Arms

Standing in Main Street from 1758, this pub was originally known as The Red Lion. Owned by the Brooke family from the early 1800s, it was sold to Greenall Whitney in about 1927. Its position in the centre of the village, close to the castle, ensured its trade was always busy. To the left, we can also see Seneschal's House, built in 1598. This is the oldest standing building in Runcorn. The word means 'steward dealing with domestic arrangements, ceremonies and the administration of justice at the castle'. First built and inhabited by the judge John King, it was latterly a farmhouse.

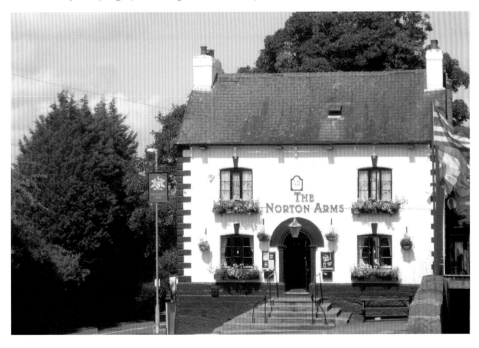

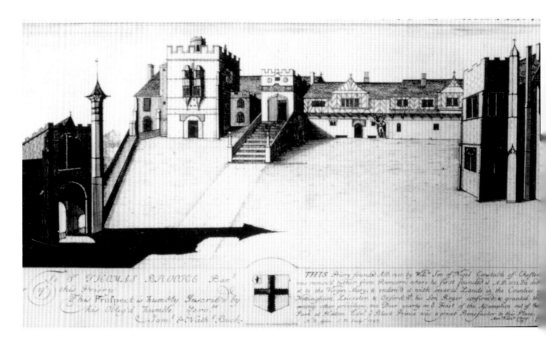

Norton Priory

In 1115, William Fitz Nigel, 2nd Baron Halton, founded an Augustinian priory in Runcorn. In 1134, his son, William Fitz William, moved the priory to a more favourable site at Norton, in the shadow of the castle. In the early years, the barons were generous benefactors, and the priory was enlarged to become a large community. By the early sixteenth century, the priory was falling into financial problems. The Dissolution of the Monasteries by King Henry VIII saw the end of religious life in Norton. However, we can still learn and wonder by visiting the museum now on the site.

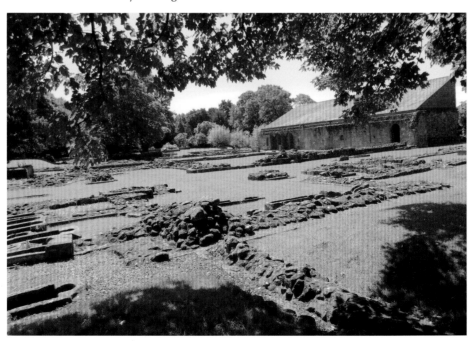

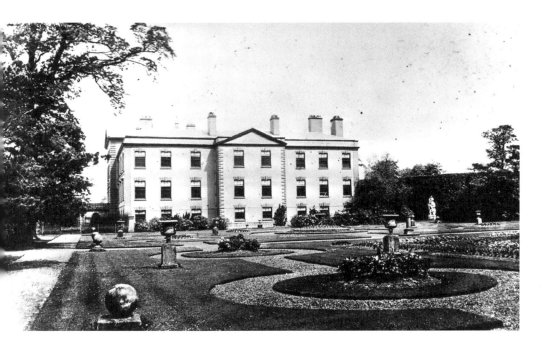

Norton Priory House

In 1545, the Manor of Norton and abbey buildings were bought for the sum of £1,500 by Richard Brooke from Leighton, near Crewe, Vice Admiral of England. In 1730, the Tudor house was replaced by a Georgian country house. Over the years, improvements were made. However, this country idyll was to be ended by the coming of the canals and industry. The family were in dispute with the Duke of Bridgewater over the route of the canal, and were displeased when their views over the Mersey were ruined by industry. In 1921, the Brooke family left Norton Priory, and the mansion was demolished in 1928. The walled garden is still lovingly cared for.

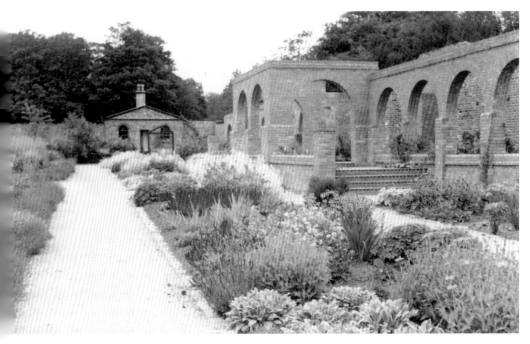

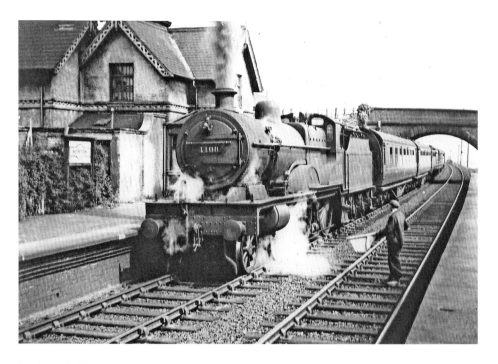

Norton Station
A view of the station in 1947. For those railway enthusiasts, I am told this is an LMS Compound wrong line working. The station first appeared in the public timetable in March 1852. It closed in 1952. With the coming of the New Town, a new facility was built slightly to the south-west. The new station was named Runcorn East and opened on 3 October 1983. The Norton station building is still in use as a private residence.

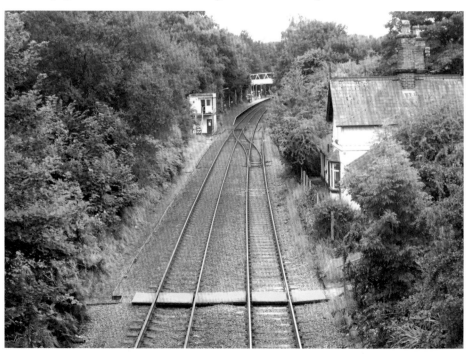

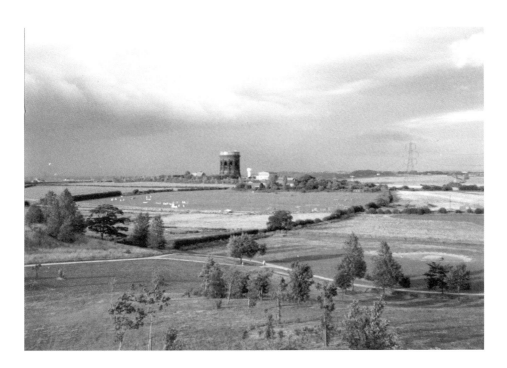

Norton Water Tower

This was built in 1892 as a balancing reservoir on Liverpool's pipeline from Lake Vyrnwy, to ensure the expansion of local industry and to provide water to Runcorn. Built of Runcorn sandstone, it stands 34 metres high and holds 3,000 tons of water. Water is supplied to Liverpool by a tunnel under the River Mersey. The modern photograph is taken from Red Brow Lane, and the tower still dominates the countryside today.

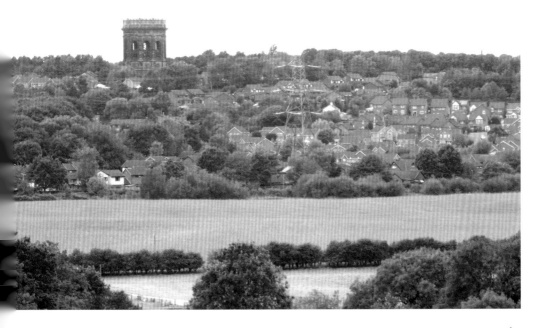

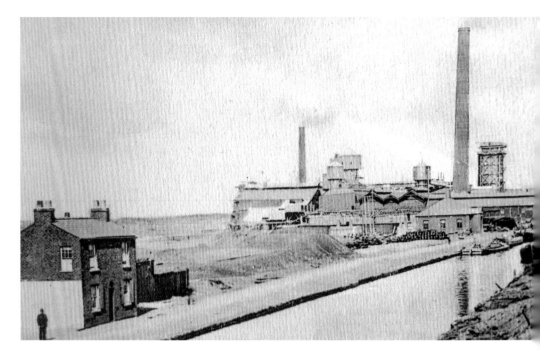

Old Quay Canal

The Old Quay canal from Runcorn to Latchford had been in decline for many years before the building of the Manchester Ship Canal. This was a boom time for Runcorn shopkeepers, but the new canal swept away many of the canalside properties. The Wigg works, however, profited from now being in deep water, and oceangoing vessels could load at the wharf. This area is being transformed once more, with the building of the second Mersey crossing.

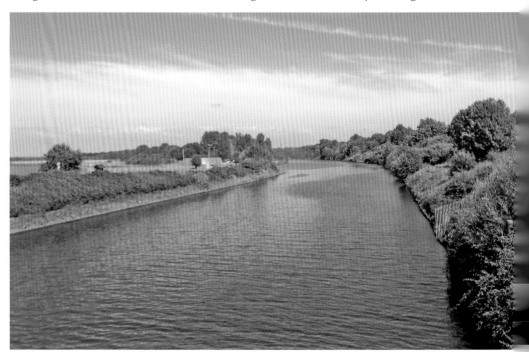

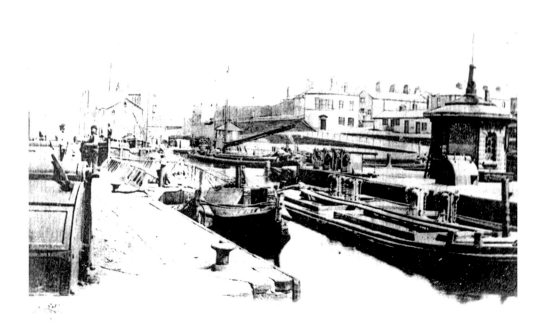

Old Quay Docks

From around 1869, the maritime trade industry was increasing. We see Old Quay Docks busy with sailing flats and coastal schooners. The coming of the Manchester Ship Canal saw the demise of the Old Quay Docks. The Old Quay Mill, offices and wharfs were swept away, having stood for 200 years. The canal wall made it impossible to launch large vessels from the slipway. Happily, ship repair work was not lost completely as the Manchester Ship Canal Company established its tug boat depot here.

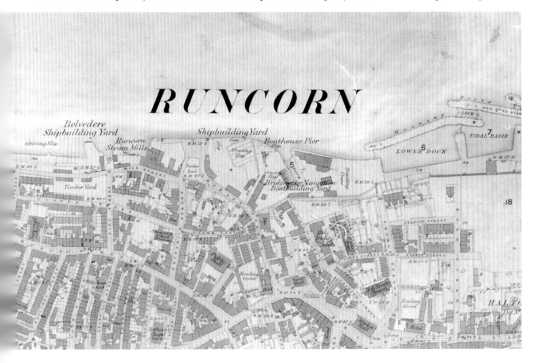

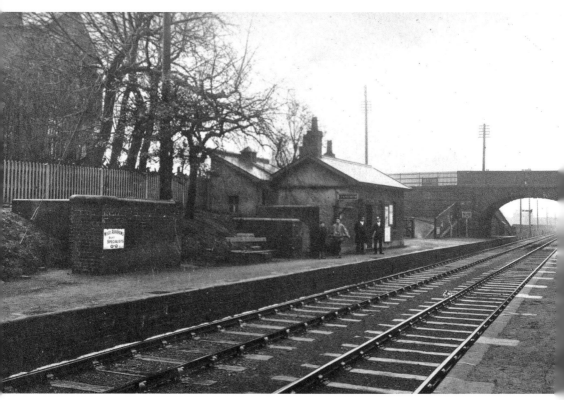

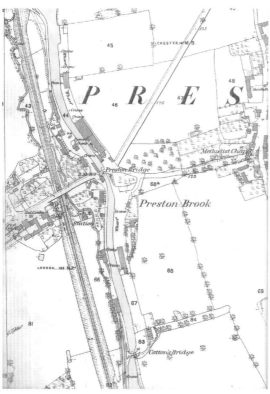

Preston Brook Station and Preston Brook Station Hotel

The station on the Warrington – Crewe line was opened in 1837 and closed to passengers in 1948. Bagshaw's Directory of 1850 tells us that Robert Parry was the stationmaster. We can see the station, on this map of 1874, and the busy wharfs alongside the canal. Bagshaw's Directory tells us there was a bus from the Red Lion Hotel daily, at 1.30 p.m. The Greenall family owned it from 1892. The hotel was later run by the Whitlow family, who were farmers in the village, for many years. It was a busy hotel standing on the main road between Chester and Warrington and catering for railway passengers. It closed in the 1990s following a fire.

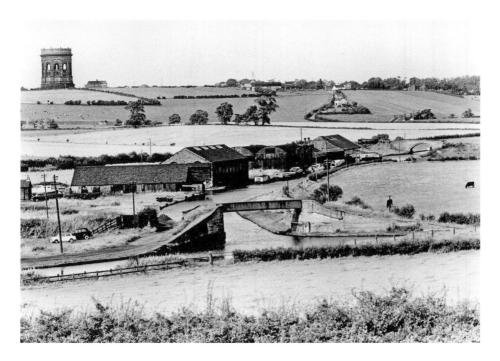

Preston Brook Waters Meeting

The junction of the Bridgewater, the Trent and Mersey Canal. In 1761, James Brindley visited Runcorn to survey the route of the Bridgewater Canal. Richard Brooke, the landowner, proved to be the Nimby of his time by challenging the route for many years. It was 1776 before the canal was completed to Manchester. In 1766, the Trent and Mersey canal joined up at Preston Brook. This opened up communications with the Midlands.

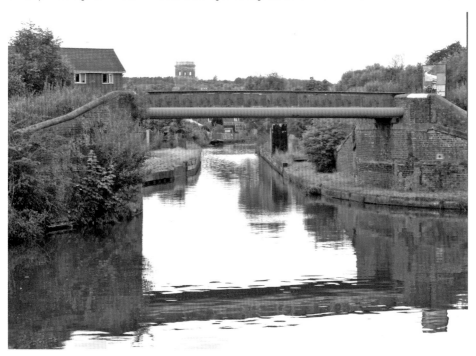

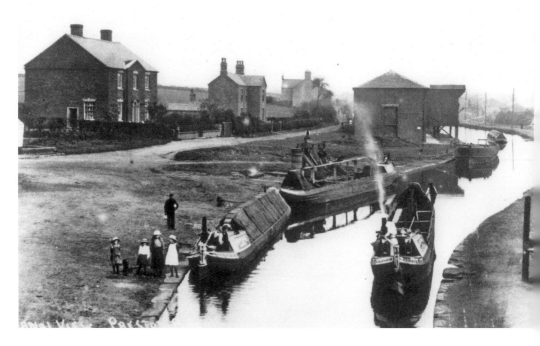

Preston Brook Barges and Warehouses
Preston Brook was very busy with warehouses and cranes loading and unloading. Coal arrived from Worsley, pottery arrived from Stoke, and barges would return with china, clay and stone.

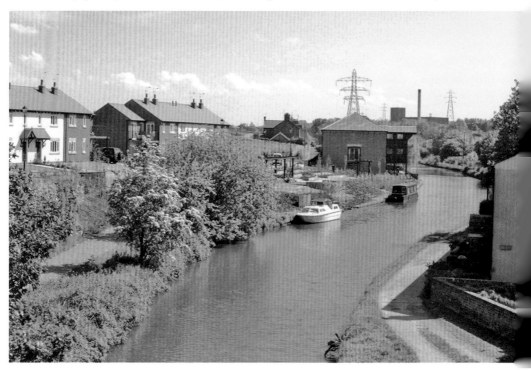

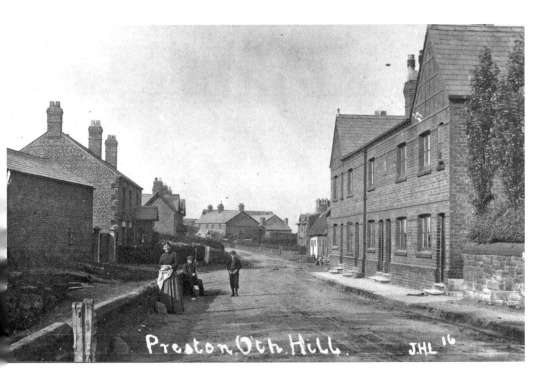

Preston on the Hill

Windmill Lane in the early 1900s. The houses on the right were built by the Greenall family in 1893. The village was formerly known as Preston juxta Dutton. It was in the possession of the Duttons of Dutton Hall. John Wesley preached at a house opposite in 1781 and 1783, and the Methodist chapel was later built on the site. The village became a stronghold of primitive Methodism.

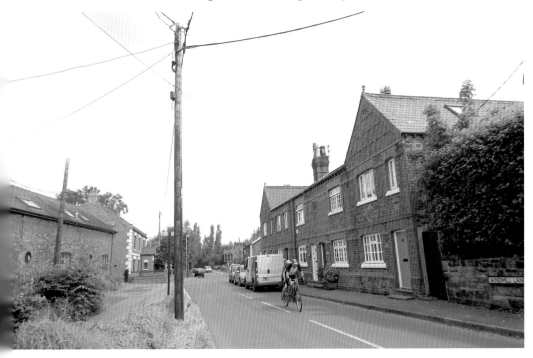

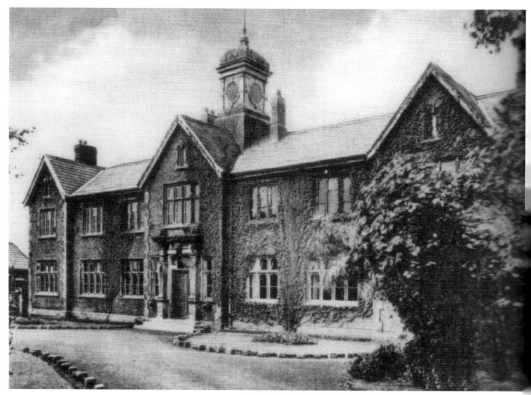

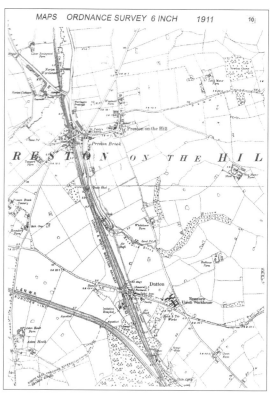

Runcorn Workhouse

Often known as Dutton Workhouse, it was built in 1857 by the Runcorn Poor Law Union. It was designed to accommodate 232 people. It was used as a wartime hospital in the 1940s. Although described as a handsome brick structure, entering here would have filled the inmates with dread. It is worth remembering, though, if you find your ancestor residing here in the census, that it was not only poverty that brought people here. This was the only place to receive free healthcare before the NHS. It was demolished around 1975. Here we can see the map of 1911.

Rocksavage

Built of local red sandstone in 1568 by Sir John Savage. The impressive front of Rocksavage had two great octagonal, towers surmounted with domes and bridged by a castellated wall to create an imposing entrance. The house was vast, and stood in formal Elizabethan gardens. It was sited so as to command views across the Weaver valley towards Frodsham, the Welsh hills and beyond. In 1617, King James I and his entourage were entertained at Rocksavage. Only a few walls remain.

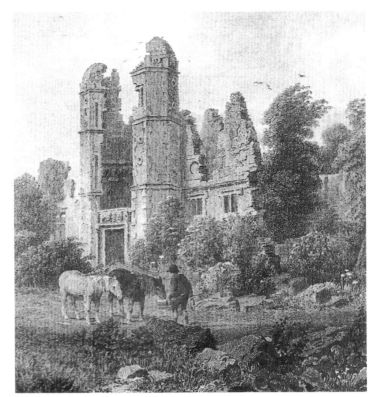

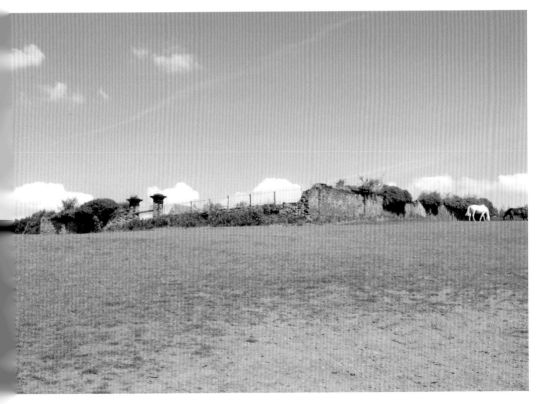

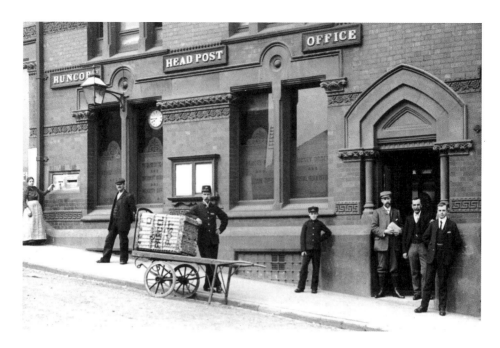

Runcorn Post Office

The head post office in Victoria Buildings in Devonshire Place. There had also been a post office on High Street and later in Bank Chambers on High Street. The service was excellent. Kelly's Directory of 1902 shows the postmaster as William Bennett. The post office was open from 7.00 a.m.–9.00 p.m. There were four deliveries of letters: 7.00 a.m., 8.00 a.m., 14.15 p.m. and 16.20 p.m. On Sunday there is only one delivery, commencing at 7.00 a.m. Can you imagine a service like that today! The fine building still stands proudly on the corner. If you look closely, you can see the post box to the left.

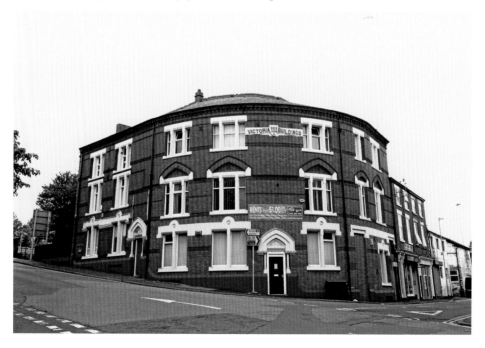

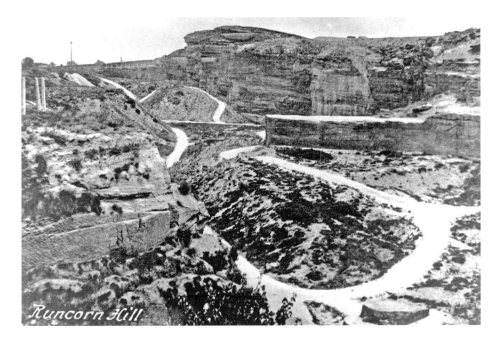

Runcorn Hill

Quarrying was being undertaken on the hill around Highlands Road as early as 1819. Demand for the excellent pink and red keuper sandstone grew, and the industry flourished. The stone graces many fine buildings in the North West, including Chester Cathedral, St Georges Hall, Liverpool, and Holker Hall in Cumbria. The easy access to the wharf at Weston was a factor. Workers came from Wales and Cumbria to work in the quarries. As the quarries gradually disappeared, the old tunnels were put to good use as air raid shelters in the Second World War. We now see the Frodsham Silver Band concert on a sunny Sunday.

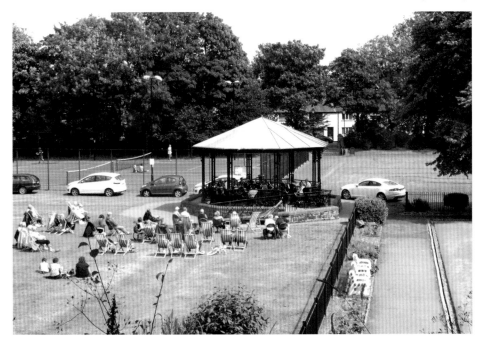

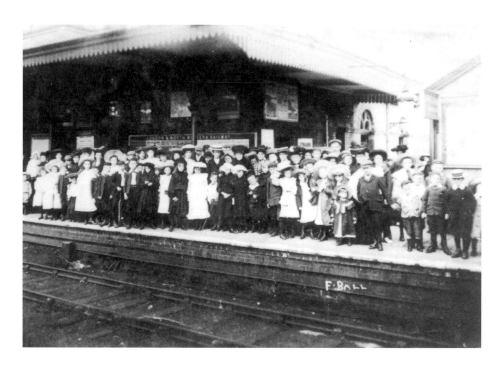

Runcorn Railway Station

The original Runcorn station was on the Chester – Warrington line. The station opened on 1 April 1869. Here we see a crowd of excited families on a day trip to the seaside in 1900. In September 1915, *The Manchester Guardian* reported the sad death of the stationmaster Mr John Bryden. He was signalling to a Northwich train when the *London Express* emerged from the tunnel and hit him. The station has recently been modernised, and a large multi-storey car park has been provided.

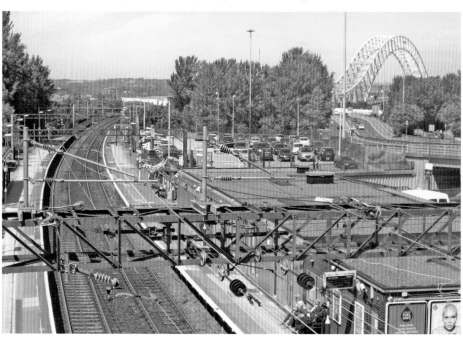

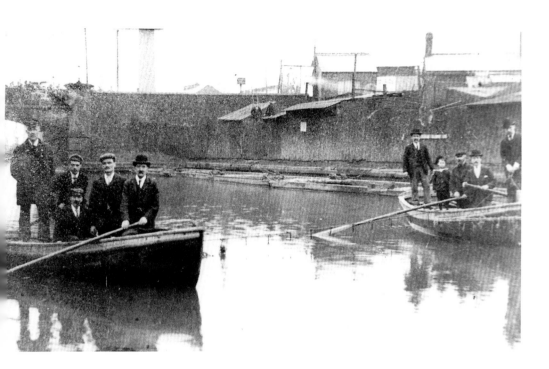

Runcorn Widnes Grappling Corps

The river and canals of Runcorn were dangerous, and death by drowning was a frequent occurrence. The Runcorn Grappling Corps were founded in 1901. They gave some solace to grieving families by recovering bodies from the water. It was a volunteer organisation that relied on local people for funds. Sadly, *The Manchester Guardian* of May 1914 reported that Mr William Byfield, founder of the Corps, fell from his cycle in Stockton Health and was killed. This photograph looks to have been taken close to Camden works. The canal is now a much greener, tranquil scene.

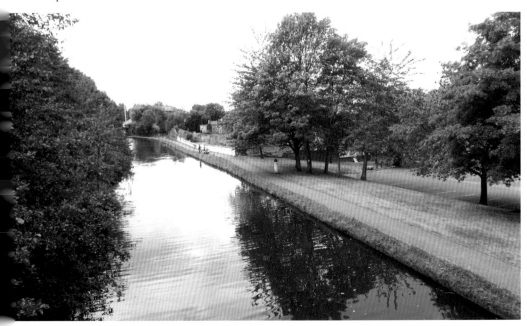

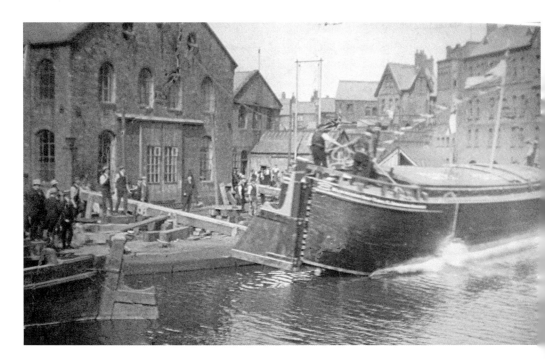

Sprinch Boatyard

This boatyard on the Bridgewater Canal had a fine reputation, and was responsible for the maintenance of over 200 canal craft. Two centuries of traditional shipbuilding were lost when the approach road to the new bridge was built in 1962. The Sprinch brook was the Runcorn's first water supply. It originally flowed across the road near the Royal Hotel. It was culverted to serve the fountain outside the police station in Bridge Street.

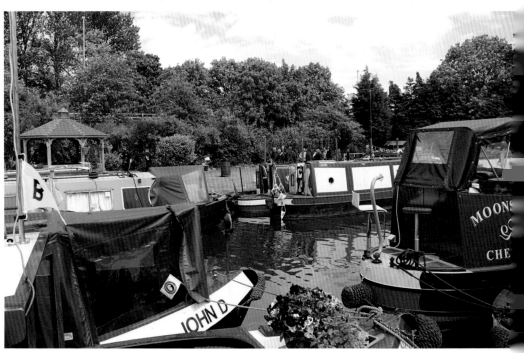

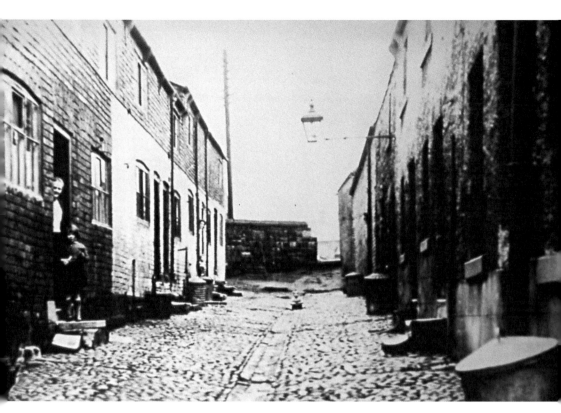

Stone Street off Bridge Street
A view of Mrs Caulfield standing
on the steps of her cottage. Mrs
Caulfield also owned the others
in the row, and rented them out
to boat people from the canal
for 5s a week. It was known as
Treacle Row. To the right, we see
the map of 1874 showing Stone
Street, the gasworks and the
Victoria boatyard.

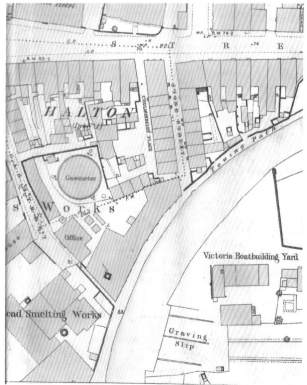

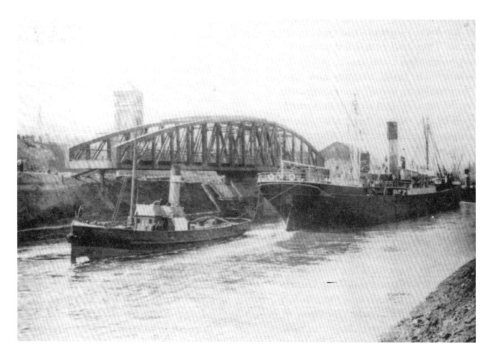

Old Quay Swing Bridge

Built around 1894, this swing bridge over the Manchester Ship Canal links the town with Wigg Island. It is operated from the south bank of the canal by means of a hydraulic system. This is operated from machinery in a group of three slate-roofed, red-brick buildings, an engine house, an accumulator tower and the control building. Thankfully, it still stands today and is well worth a visit. You may be lucky enough to see it swing.

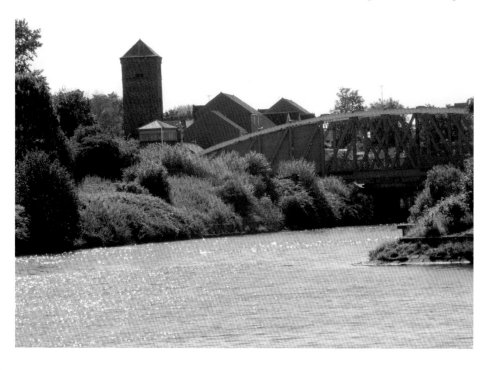

Theatre Royal

Duke Street, built in 1869, held 1,200 people. Being made of wood, it was vulnerable and was destroyed by fire in 1906. Here we see crowds viewing the spectacle. *The Manchester Guardian* of 10 July 1906 reported 'at 16.30 the theatre was found to be on fire by 17.00, it was a heap of ruins'. The map shows its position on the corner of Wellington Street and Duke Street.

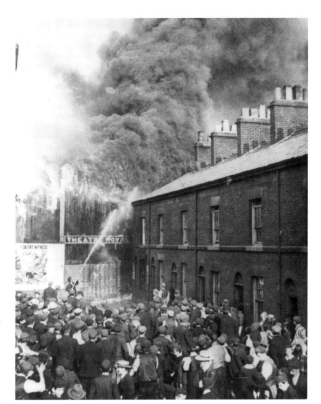

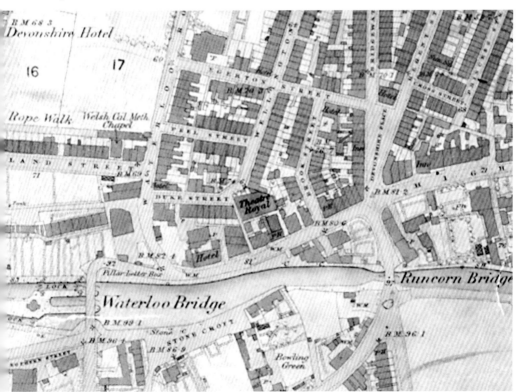

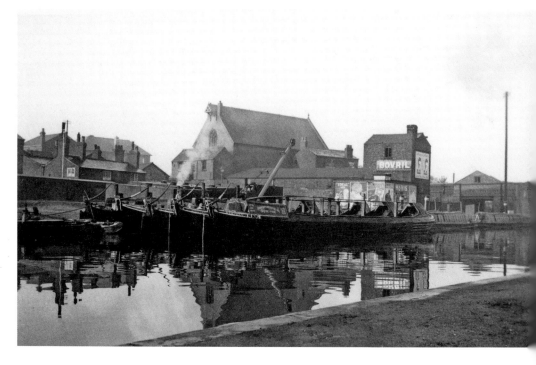

Top Locks

The first of the locks before travelling down to the Mersey. An approach road to the Runcorn–Widnes Bridge was built in 1960, blocking the line of the locks immediately behind Waterloo Bridge. The modern photograph shows a different view towards the High Street. The Waterloo Hotel is now closed.

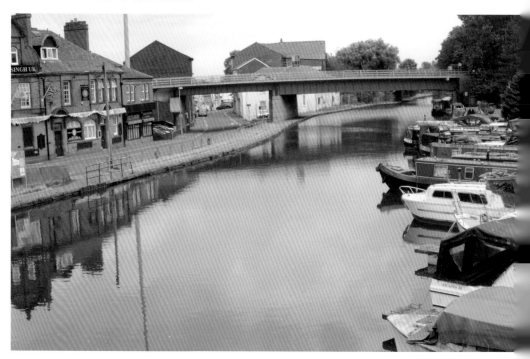

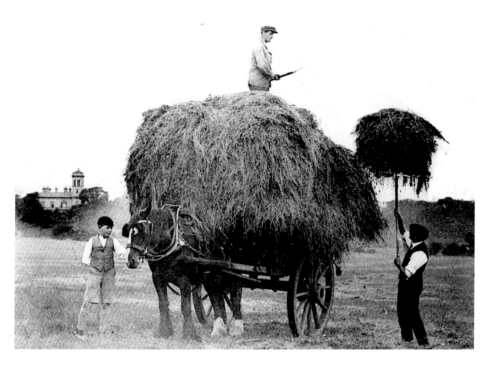

The Town Hall

The hall was built in 1856. In 1932, the council purchased Halton Grange, the former home of Thomas Johnson, and later the Hazlehurst family. It was sold by Francis Boston for £2,250 plus 12 acres of land. Here we see a very rural scene. The town hall gardens now provide a lovely green setting.

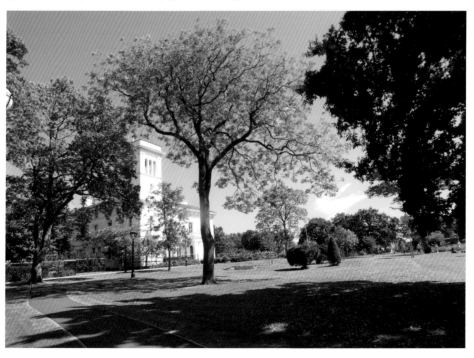

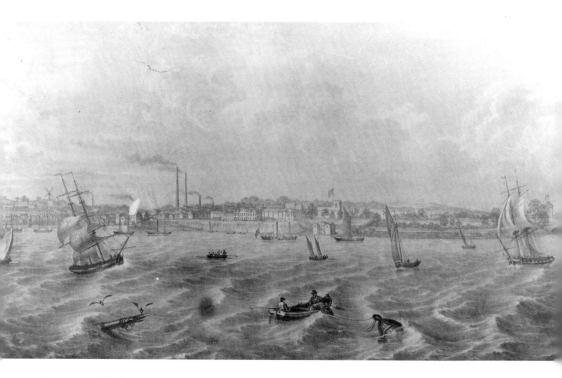

Runcorn Old View

A view from 1840, with steamers leaving the old quay docks. We can see the original medieval church, the windmill and the saltwater baths, built in 1822 when Runcorn was a resort town and visitors came to take the waters. We can see industrial Runcorn emerging with Johnson's and Hazlehurst's chimneys. These chimneys were quite a landmark, standing so high.

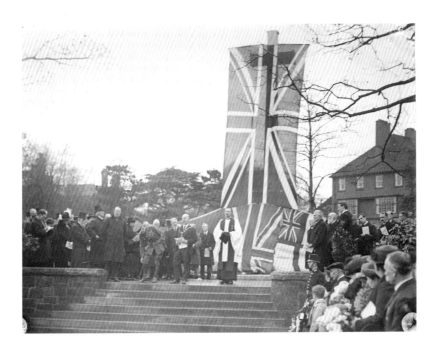

War Memorial

The war memorial was unveiled on 14 November 1920, and was rededicated following the Second World War with additional name panels on 7 November 1948. It has been updated since. Looking on the Commonwealth Graves Commission website, we can see Robert Llewellyn Douglas, aged twenty-three, son of Llewellyn Douglas of No.1 Cawley Street, Runcorn, is commemorated at Ypres, and Thomas Eaton Fowler, aged twenty, son of William and Sarah Fowler of Runcorn, is buried at Les Baraques Cemetery in France. They are just two of the brave Runcorn men who lost their lives in the First World War. The modern photograph was taken at the service of commemoration in August 2014.

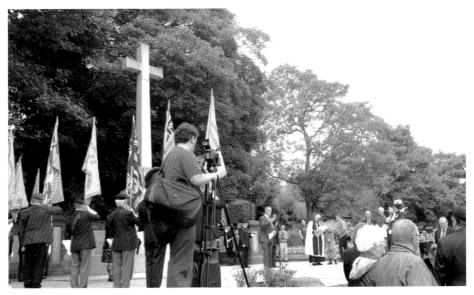

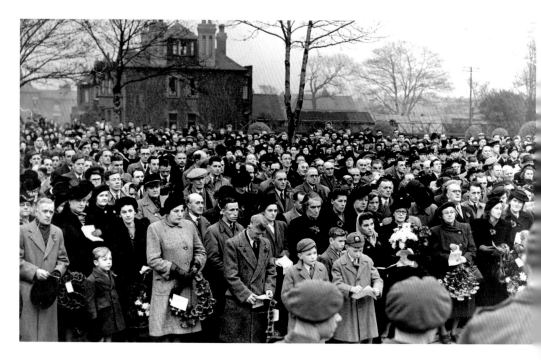

War Memorial, 1949

A moving photograph, as this was 1949 and war was still vivid in people's memories. Many of those standing will have lost sons, daughters and parents to the war. Roy Gough tells me that the two boys in the front, wearing school caps, are brothers Derek & Bernard McCann, both now sadly passed away. The modern photograph, again, shows the ceremony held at the memorial gardens in August and the unveiling of Todger Jones's statue.

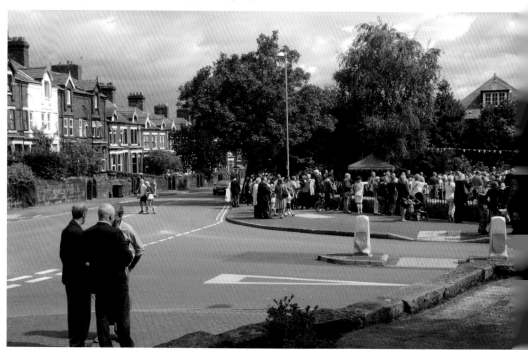

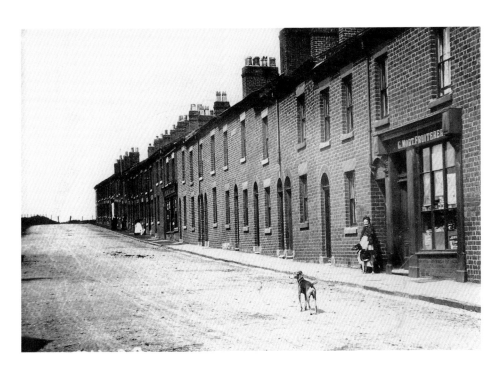

Weston Heath Road

In 1801, there were only 162 inhabitants in Weston Village. The chemical works and the quarries increased this by 2,115 in 1901. The 1873 map shows the road as Weston Terrace. The 1914 directory shows Margaret Mort, shopkeeper at No. 6, and also Mrs Elizabeth Mort, grocer at No. 66.

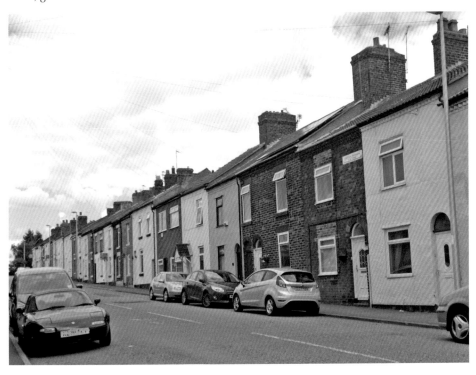

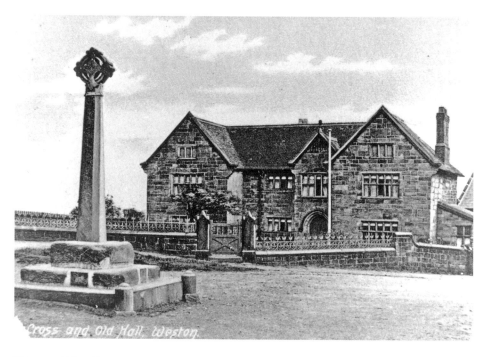

Weston Old Hall

Originally built in 1607, but altered and restored many times. Although originally a farmhouse, it is built in grand style of Runcorn sandstone, with four bays and mullion windows. The manor belonged to Major G. Orred. The 1847 tithe map shows Ann Orred owning much of the land in Weston.The family donated £500 towards the building of Saint John's school chapel. The Bankes family were also major landowners and worked Overhill Farm.

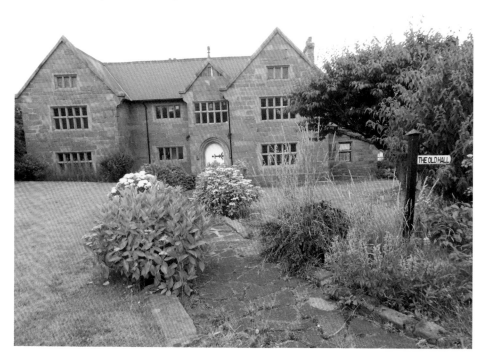

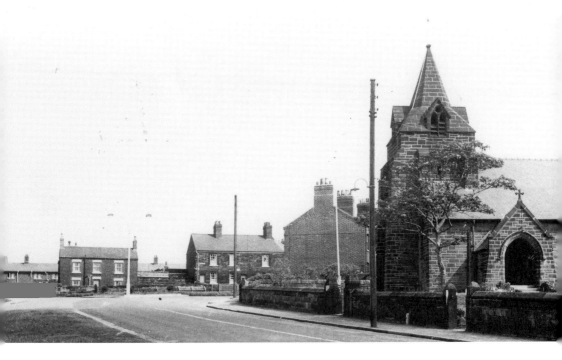

Weston Village

Saint John's church is built from local sandstone. The church is known as the Choirboys' church. In the 1890s, the curate organised the boys to write letters to choirs worldwide and to prominent people to request money to build their church. The church was built in 1898. The choirboys' initials were carved on the steeple, and can still be seen today.

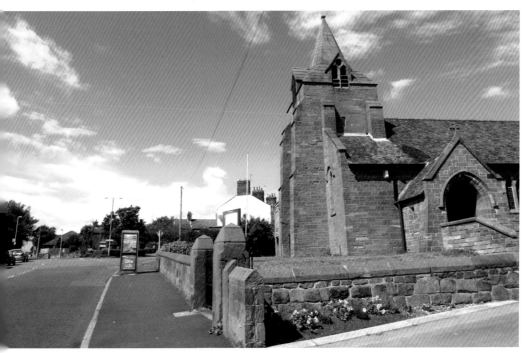

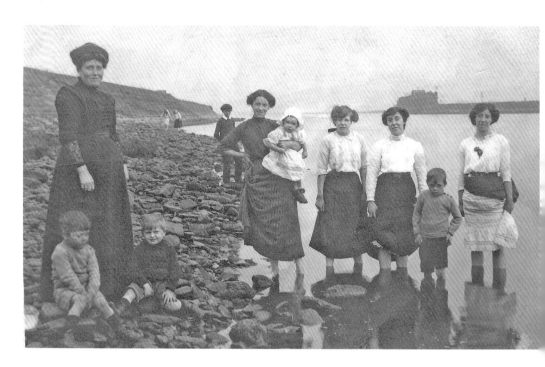

Weston Point Bathing

A charming photograph of 'bathing belles' at stony wall, a popular spot on sunny days. The stone wall was shaped from broken sandstone forming a small sandy bay on the banks of the Ship Canal. It was safe to paddle, but the more adventurous would swim across the canal, which was a rather dangerous trip, given how busy the shipping lanes were. There are no bathers now, but hopefully the coastline here will be busy with shipping again soon.

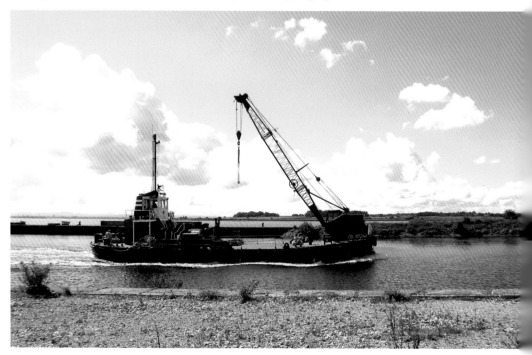

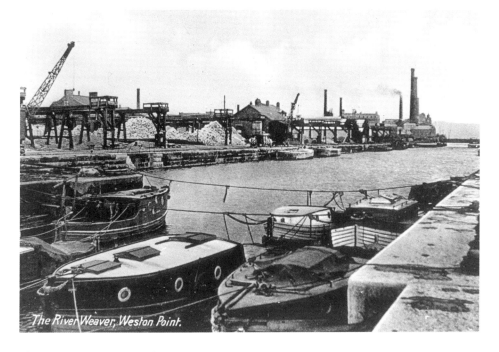

The River Weaver, Weston Point.

River Weaver, Weston Point

The Cheshire salt trade required improvements to the river to make it navigable. These were authorised in 1720. The Weaver formerly joined the River Mersey at Weston Marsh, but since the construction of the Manchester Ship Canal, it now flows via Weaver Navigation into the canal. In August 2007, the port became the property of The Stobart Group. We can now see the new warehousing, and hopefully the port will live again.

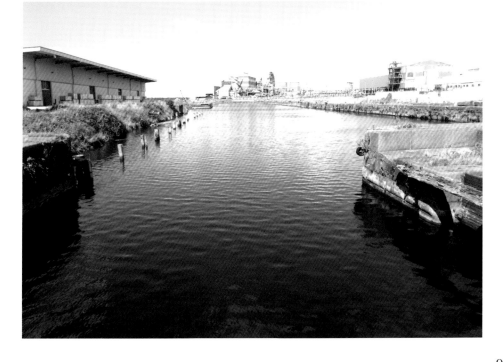

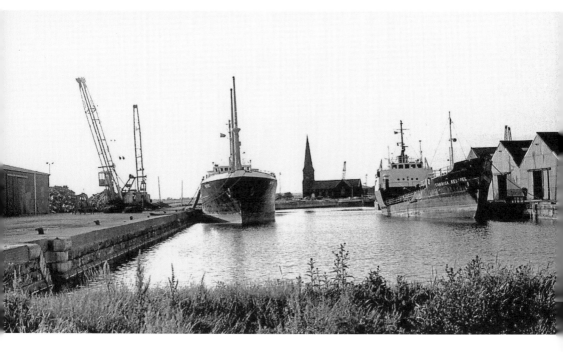

Weston Point and Church

The Island church was built in 1841 by the River Weaver Navigation Co. to serve their employees. A school was built for the boatmen's families. The church was called Christ church and stood on a headland jutting into the Mersey. The building of the Manchester Ship Canal resulted in the church sitting on an island. The church was well loved by the people of Weston Point, and it is much regretted that it is now closed.

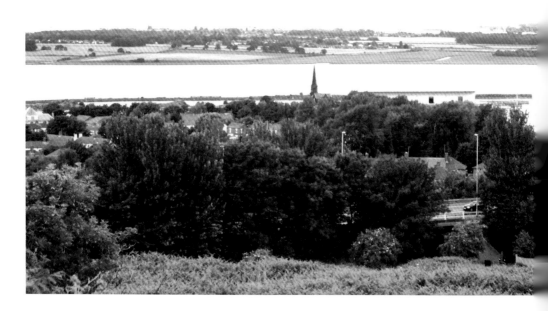

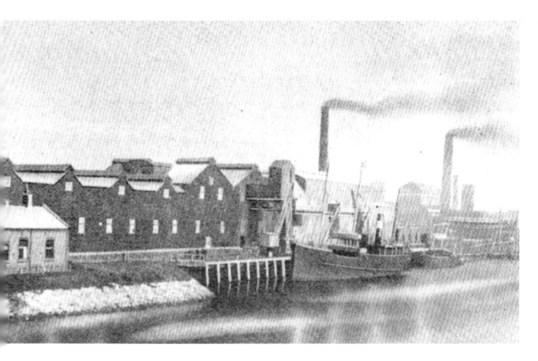

Wigg Works

The island is named after Charles Wigg, who started an alkali works here in the 1860s to extract copper from its core. It was originally known as Quay Old Chemical Works and later as Randles. It was first served by the Runcorn–Latchford Canal, and later by the Manchester Ship Canal. During the Second World War, it became notorious for the production of mustard gas. After the war, it was operated by ICI, but production ended in the 1960s. Wigg Island is now a local nature reserve, opened by the mayor of Halton and Bill Oddie on 19 April 2002. This is all that is left of the once busy wharf.

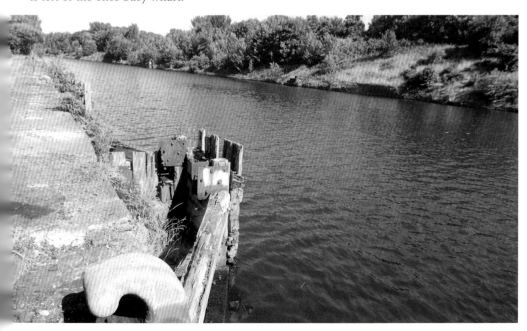

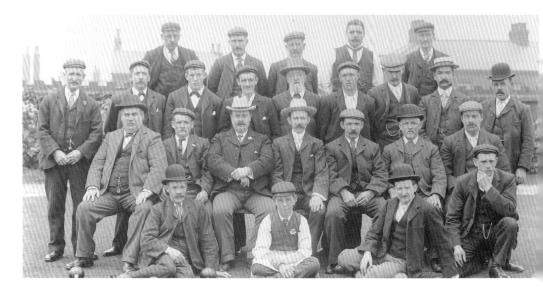

Wilson's Bowling Club

The Wilson's is one of the oldest pubs in Runcorn, and was built over 300 years ago. It was known as the Bowling Green Inn, before Job Wilson took it over in 1805. Binge drinking was a problem even then; in 1806 a meeting was held in the pub to propose a bridewell where drunkards could sleep it off. The bowling green was opened in 1911. It is also said to be haunted, with a dashing young cavalier who is sometimes seen walking through the upstairs room of the old inn. *Back row left to right*: J. Lightfoot, B. Jolley, J. Ellams, J. Wildgoose, W. Banner. *Second row*: J. Faulkner, T. Warder, A. Moulton, G. Banner, R. Wright, S. Johnson, R. Wilson, T. Bebbington, T. Chamberlain. *Third row*: F. Jolley, T. Riley, A. Torril, E. Turner, C. Woods, W. Copper, S. Houghton. *Front row*: H. Nickson, R. Wildgoose, F. Rawlinson, T. Wilkinson.

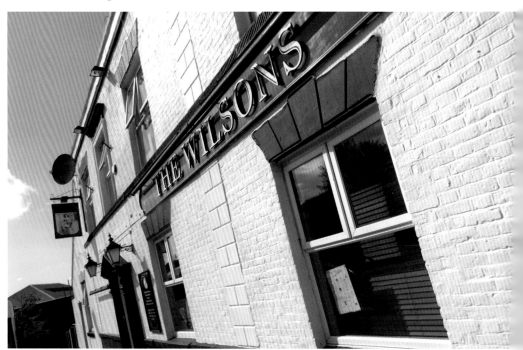